The Retirement Instinct

The Reflex That Makes You Afraid to Spend the Money You Saved

Jordan Ellis

First edition, 2026

Published by Jordan Ellis

Contents

Foreword

I've watched people spend thirty years doing something genuinely hard — saving on purpose, month after month, past the point where it was comfortable — and then, the moment they were finally allowed to stop and use the money, freeze. Not run out. Not lose it. Freeze, with more than enough sitting right there, unable to spend it on the life it was supposedly for.

I didn't expect that to be the pattern. I expected retirement to be the easy chapter, the reward at the end of a much harder book. What I kept hearing instead, from people who by any honest measure had done everything right, was a specific kind of quiet distress that had nothing to do with the numbers. The math worked. The advisor had run it three ways and said, in writing, that they could spend more. And still, somehow, the withdrawals didn't happen, or happened smaller than planned, or came with a private guilt no spreadsheet could talk them out of.

That's not the same problem this library has already covered. It isn't lifestyle creep, which is about money leaking out faster than it should. It isn't a lifelong habit of living tight regardless of circumstance, which is a standing trait with no particular starting gun. This is narrower, and it has an exact starting gun: the day the paycheck stops. Not gradually. Not as a mood. As an event — the specific week the income that has arrived, reliably, for decades, simply doesn't arrive anymore, and the account that used to fill now, for the first time in a working life, only empties.

I wrote this book because that week deserves its own name, and because almost nobody carrying this fear has one for it. They call it caution. They call it being careful. Some of them call it, sadly, just who they are now. It isn't who they are. It's a reflex, installed by decades of a system that only knew how to defend a rising number, meeting a life stage that finally asks it to defend a falling one instead. The reflex doesn't know the difference. This book is for the people ready to teach it.

— Jordan Ellis

Introduction

There is a specific moment, arriving for almost everyone who saves diligently enough to retire on their own terms, when the direction of the money reverses — and something in the saver doesn't reverse with it.

For decades, the entire architecture of a working financial life points one way. A paycheck arrives. Some of it gets spent, and some of it, if the saver has been disciplined, gets set aside — into an account, a fund, a plan, growing slowly across years by the simple accumulation of contribution after contribution, aided along by markets doing what markets do over long enough stretches of time. The number goes up. Not every month, not every year, but on the whole, across a working life, the pattern is unmistakable: the account grows. And a saver's nervous system, over enough decades of watching that number rise, comes to associate a rising number with safety, and — this is the part that matters — comes to associate the account itself with the specific, deeply reinforced act of contribution. Depositing money into that account isn't just a financial behavior. It becomes, for many people, one of the load-bearing habits of their entire identity. Disciplined. Responsible. The one who didn't spend it all. The one who thought ahead.

Then, on a specific day — a retirement date, a last day of work, sometimes a layoff that becomes a retirement sooner than planned — the paycheck stops. Not the money. The paycheck. The reliable, recurring, external deposit that has arrived on a schedule for thirty or forty years, the deposit that made saving feel almost automatic because there was always more coming behind it, simply ends. And the account that spent decades being fed now has to start being drawn from, for the first time in the saver's adult life, with nothing behind it refilling the tank. The direction of the money, for the first time in decades, runs the other way.

Here is the master thesis this entire book is built to earn: *the fear of spending retirement savings is not a fear about running out of money — it's the nervous system's reaction to losing the income source that used to make spending feel safe, and the withdrawal itself gets coded as loss even when the plan says otherwise, because the system defending your money was never built to defend a number that's supposed to fall.* This is not a character flaw. It is not evidence that you secretly don't trust yourself, or that you're more anxious than other people, or that something is wrong with your relationship to money in some deep, unfixable way. It's a mismatch between a system built for one direction and a life stage that requires the opposite direction, and mismatches like that are fixable the moment you can see them clearly for what they are.

It's worth being precise, immediately, about how this differs from a pattern this library has already covered — the standing, lifelong habit of living tight regardless of circumstance, the kind of chronic underspending that shows up whether or not there's a specific reason for it, present in someone's twenties as readily as their eighties. That pattern is a trait. It doesn't need an event to trigger it; it's simply how a person relates to money, day in and day out, across an entire adult life, often traceable to an early experience of real scarcity that never got updated. What this book is about is different in a way that matters enormously for how you fix it. This is not a lifelong trait. It's a reflex that activates at a specific transition — the loss of the income source — in people who often had a perfectly normal, even relaxed, relationship with spending for their entire working life right up until the week the paycheck stopped. A person can spend easily, generously, without a second thought, for thirty-five years of earning, and then discover, the month after their last paycheck clears, that their hand won't move to authorize a withdrawal from an account holding more money than they will realistically ever need. That's not who they've always been. That's who the transition made them, on a specific and identifiable date, and dates are useful precisely because what happens on a date can be traced, examined, and eventually undone.

Consider what actually changes, mechanically, on the day the paycheck stops, because the change is more total than most people register in the moment. For decades, every dollar spent had, behind it, an implicit promise: more is coming. A vacation charged to a credit card in March gets quietly backstopped by the paycheck landing in April. A larger-than-usual grocery bill barely registers, because the next deposit is already scheduled, already guaranteed, already accounted for in a part of the mind that doesn't need to consciously calculate it. That backstop is not a minor comfort. It is, functionally, the entire reason spending during a working life feels as easy as it usually does — not because working people are careless with money, but because every dollar spent is quietly guaranteed to be replaced. Retirement removes the guarantee. The account you're now living from is, for the vast majority of retirees, a fixed pool rather than a replenishing stream, and every dollar drawn from a fixed pool is, for the first time in that person's adult life, actually and permanently gone in a way no dollar spent during the working years ever quite was. The mind notices this shift long before the conscious self does, and it reacts the way minds react to a genuinely new category of risk: with caution that can tip, unaddressed, into paralysis.

This book exists because that paralysis is common, expensive, and almost never named accurately. People experiencing it tend to describe it to themselves as prudence — a virtue, something to be proud of, evidence of the same discipline that built the account in the first place. And there is real prudence involved in a well-run retirement; this book is not an argument for recklessness, and nothing in it will tell you to ignore an honest number your own plan actually can't support.

But there is a specific, identifiable population of retirees — likely including you, if this book found its way into your hands — whose actual, verified financial plan supports meaningfully more spending than they're currently doing, sometimes by a wide margin, and whose refusal to spend it isn't caution at all. It's a reflex defending an old rule — the rule that governed thirty years of accumulation — in a season of life that rule was never built for.

There's a term economists have used for decades to describe the strange gap between what the standard theory of lifetime spending predicts retirees will do and what retirees actually, empirically, do. The foundational theory — developed by the economist Franco Modigliani, working with Richard Brumberg, in the 1950s, and later recognized with a Nobel Prize in Economic Sciences — is called the life-cycle hypothesis. It predicts, in its simplest form, that a rational saver will smooth consumption across an entire lifetime: saving during the high-income working years, then spending down savings at a fairly steady rate during retirement, aiming to arrive at the end of life with the account close to empty, since money left unspent at death represents consumption that could have improved the saver's own life and simply didn't. It's a clean, sensible model, and it describes almost nobody. What decades of subsequent research have found instead is that most retirees spend down their savings far more slowly than the theory predicts — many retirees' account balances stay roughly flat, or even continue growing, well into their seventies and eighties, long after any reasonable read of their own plan would tell them they could safely spend more. Economists studying this gap call it, informally, the retirement consumption puzzle, or sometimes the decumulation puzzle — a term for exactly the mismatch this book exists to explain. The puzzle isn't a mystery of arithmetic. Retirees generally know, roughly, what their accounts can support. The puzzle is behavioral: knowing you can spend and being able to actually do it turn out to be two entirely different systems, and this book is concerned entirely with the second one.

It helps to say clearly, before the chapters begin, what separates the reflex this book describes from ordinary financial responsibility, because the line between them can look thin from the outside and needs to be drawn honestly. Someone whose retirement plan genuinely cannot support more spending, and who is therefore living carefully out of real necessity, is not the subject of this book — that person's caution is accurate, not reflexive, and nothing here should talk them into ignoring their own numbers. The subject of this book is the retiree whose numbers, run honestly by a professional or by careful math of their own, say one thing, while their behavior says another — the retiree who has been told, explicitly, in a document they paid for, that they could spend forty percent more than they currently do and still very likely die with money left over, and who has read that document twice and changed nothing. That gap — between the verified plan and the actual behavior — is where this book lives, chapter after chapter, in its different shapes.

Those shapes vary more than you might expect from a single underlying reflex, and naming that variety is most of what the chapters ahead are for. Sometimes it looks like a budget that never loosens even after the plan says it safely could. Sometimes it looks like treating every purchase as either "necessary," and therefore permitted, or "frivolous," and therefore forbidden, with almost nothing allowed to exist in between. Sometimes it looks like a retiree who trusts their advisor's math completely and still cannot make their hand authorize the transfer the math recommends. Sometimes it looks like an ongoing, low-grade dread of catastrophe — a health crisis, a market crash, an unnamed emergency — that never quite arrives but never quite stops being planned for, either. Sometimes it looks like being able to give money away to children or grandchildren with real ease while being completely unable to spend an equivalent amount on oneself. Sometimes it isn't really about money at all on the surface — it's about a retiree who can't stop working in some form, taking on consulting projects or part-time shifts or unpaid obligations that function, whether they'd say so or not, as a way of keeping a paycheck-shaped structure alive rather than facing its absence directly. Ten chapters, ten shapes. One reflex underneath all of them, installed on the same date, defending the same old rule against a life stage built to retire it along with everything else.

It's worth addressing, briefly, a question some readers will bring to this book from personal experience with a spouse, sibling, or friend who seems to show almost no version of this reflex at all — someone who retired and simply, easily, started spending at the level their plan supported, without any of the hesitation this book spends ten chapters describing. That variation is real, and it's worth flagging honestly rather than implying every retiree experiences this pattern to some meaningful degree. People whose sense of identity was never especially tied to their earning role, whose relationship with money was calibrated by a family of origin that treated saving and spending as equally unremarkable facts of life, or who simply built a habit of regular, deliberate spending throughout their working years rather than pure accumulation, often transition into decumulation with comparatively little friction. This book isn't arguing that the reflex is universal or inevitable. It's arguing that where it does show up — and it shows up often enough to justify ten chapters of close attention — it deserves a name, a mechanism, and a set of concrete responses, rather than being left to masquerade as either an admirable virtue or a personal, unexplainable quirk.

It's worth being honest about a reasonable objection before it can quietly undermine every chapter that follows: isn't some caution in retirement simply sensible? Isn't underspending, if it has to err in one direction, obviously the safer error compared to running out of money at eighty-five with decades of life still ahead? This objection deserves a straight answer rather than a dismissal, because it's not wrong on its face. Underspending is, in one narrow sense, a safer error than overspending — nobody in this book's chapters is going to end up destitute because they enjoyed a well-supported retirement too much. But "safer" and "correct" are not the same word, and the actual cost of chronic, reflexive underspending is not zero just because it's quieter than the cost of running out. A retirement spent in genuine deprivation — skipping the visit to grandchildren because the flight feels irresponsible, letting a home repair go undone past the point of comfort, declining the medical procedure that would meaningfully improve quality of life because the number on the estimate feels too large to authorize, even when the plan can easily absorb it — is not a safe retirement. It's a retirement quietly spent guarding a number instead of living a life, and the years lost to that guarding do not come back, no matter how healthy the account balance looks at the end of them. This book takes that cost as seriously as it takes the cost of running out, because only one of those two risks gets any airtime in ordinary financial conversation, and the other one, this book's actual subject, has been left almost entirely unnamed.

It's worth being specific, too, about what this book is not attempting, so expectations are calibrated honestly from the start. This is not a book about how much you should withdraw, what withdrawal strategy best protects a portfolio, what accounts to draw from in what order, or any other question that belongs to a financial advisor with access to your actual numbers. Those are important questions, and this book has no opinion on them, deliberately — every reader's real financial capacity is different, and a book has no business pretending to know yours. What this book has an opinion on, and a fairly firm one, is the psychology sitting between a sound plan and the behavior that plan is supposed to produce. If your advisor has told you that you can safely spend more, and you haven't, this book is concerned with the gap between those two facts — not with correcting the plan, but with understanding, and eventually loosening, whatever is holding you back from living inside it.

Each chapter ahead follows the same shape, for the same reason every book in this library does: the shape is what turns an abstract psychological mechanism into something you can actually recognize and interrupt in your own life. First, a close scene or two — someone at the specific moment this chapter's version of the reflex is firing, drawn as a composite rather than a report of any real individual, built to be recognizable rather than biographical. Then the actual mechanism underneath it, named honestly and drawn from real, citable research — never invented, never dressed up to sound more authoritative than the underlying science supports. Then an honest accounting of the cost, counted in more than the dollars left unspent. Then a set of overrides — concrete, specific, psychological rather than procedural, things you can actually do the next time you feel the pull, never a product recommendation or an account instruction, because this book has no way of knowing which accounts you hold and no business pretending otherwise. And a rule, short enough to carry with you into the exact moment you'll need it, because that moment tends to arrive fast and offer very little warning.

You will very likely recognize more than one chapter as your own, and that's expected rather than unusual — the reflex this book describes doesn't confine itself to a single channel any more than any of the reflexes described elsewhere in this library do. Someone who can't loosen their monthly budget may also be quietly working a part-time job that has nothing to do with needing the income. Someone who can give money away to a grandchild with total ease may still be unable to book the trip they've wanted for a decade. Read for the chapters that land. Don't be surprised if it's most of them.

It's worth pausing, before the chapters begin, on a question that tends to arrive early for readers of this particular book, more so than for some other volumes in this library: why does this transition, specifically, land so much harder for some retirees than for others, even among people who saved comparably well and received comparably sound advice? Part of the answer lies in something touched on already — the length and consistency of the accumulation habit itself. A person who spent forty consistent years contributing to the same account, watching the same rule prove itself correct year after year, has a far more deeply grooved version of that rule to overcome than someone whose saving was less continuous, more varied, or arrived later in life through a windfall or an inheritance rather than decades of payroll deduction. The forty-year saver isn't worse at this transition because of some personal failing. They're worse at it, in a specific and almost mechanical sense, because the habit being asked to reverse is simply older, more automatic, and more thoroughly reinforced than a habit built over a shorter or less consistent stretch of time.

A second part of the answer concerns how directly a person's sense of identity was tied to the specific act of earning, as distinct from the money itself. Two retirees can hold identical account balances and experience this reflex with wildly different intensity, depending on how much of their private sense of competence, worth, and daily structure was bound up in the earning process rather than simply in its result. Someone whose career was, for them, mostly a means to an end — a job that funded a life focused elsewhere, on family, hobbies, or community — tends to experience a comparatively gentler version of the identity disruption this book describes in later chapters, because retiring doesn't remove the actual center of their identity, only one of its supports. Someone whose career was, for them, closer to the center of who they understood themselves to be experiences something closer to a genuine identity rupture on top of the purely financial transition, and the two effects compound rather than simply adding.

A third factor worth stating plainly plainly, because it's rarely discussed openly: how a person's family or culture of origin talked about money during childhood shapes not just whether they save, but how they'll eventually relate to spending down what they saved, decades later, in ways that often surprise the person experiencing them. Someone raised in a household where drawing down any kind of reserve was associated, even implicitly, with failure or desperation — "we're dipping into savings" said in the tone reserved for bad news — carries that early association into a retirement where dipping into savings is not only expected but the entire structural purpose of the account. The association doesn't check whether the current circumstances match the ones it was formed under. It simply fires, the same way every reflex in this book fires, regardless of how different the actual stakes now are.

None of this is offered to sort readers into better or worse categories of saver, or to suggest that some version of this reflex is more forgivable than another. It's offered because understanding why the intensity varies is itself part of loosening it — a retiree who understands that a forty-year habit is naturally harder to reverse than a twenty-year one stops mistaking the difficulty for evidence of some deeper personal flaw, and can instead treat it as exactly what it is: a proportionate response to a proportionately larger amount of reinforcement, nothing more mysterious than that.

One last thing before the chapters begin, because it matters for how you read everything that follows: the reflex this book describes was never a flaw in your character, and it was never evidence that the discipline which built your retirement account was somehow misguided. That discipline worked. It's the entire reason there's something to draw from now. The problem isn't the discipline. It's that the discipline never got a matching set of instructions for what to do once its job was finished — because for most of a working life, nobody teaches you how to stop accumulating any more than anyone teaches you how to stop breathing. You simply were never told the account had a second phase, one that requires the opposite skill from the one you spent decades mastering. This book is that second set of instructions. Let's start with the day the direction changed, and with the much older habit that never got the memo.

Chapter 1 — The Reservoir You Built to Never Drain

A retired civil engineer stands at the edge of his own kitchen table on the first Monday of his retirement, looking at a laptop screen showing a number larger than any number he's ever personally controlled — the total of four decades of contributions, employer matches, and market growth, verified twice by a financial planner who has told him, in a report he's read three times now, that he could withdraw a comfortable, specific monthly amount for the rest of his projected lifespan and still very likely leave money behind. He built actual reservoirs for a living — spent thirty-eight years designing municipal water systems, knew intimately how a dam works, how a spillway is engineered specifically to release water on purpose, safely, by design, because a reservoir that only fills and never releases isn't a functioning reservoir at all. It's a flood risk. He knows this the way he knows almost nothing else in his professional life better. And still, that first Monday, he does not authorize the modest, plan-approved transfer his advisor set up for him to simply click and confirm. He closes the laptop instead, tells his wife he'll "look at it again this week," and doesn't open it again for eleven days.

A retired elementary school teacher, four months into retirement after twenty-nine years in the same classroom, describes the sensation to a friend as feeling, oddly, like waiting for a check that's never going to arrive. She knows, intellectually, that her pension and modest personal savings are enough — she ran the numbers herself, twice, with a worksheet from a retirement seminar the district offered the year before she left. But every Friday, for months, some part of her still glances at her bank balance the way she used to glance at it on payday, as if a deposit might be there. When it isn't — because of course it isn't, there is no more payday, there hasn't been one in months — she feels a small, specific drop, not of grief exactly, closer to disorientation, the particular vertigo of a habit reaching for something that's stopped being there. She responds to that vertigo, without quite deciding to, by tightening her spending that week, every week, as if caution could somehow summon the missing deposit back into existence.

A retired postal supervisor offers a third version of the same reflex, quieter than the other two and, in its own way, more telling, because nothing about his situation involves any real complexity at all. His pension alone, verified by a fee-only planner he pays by the hour specifically so there's no incentive on either side to recommend anything, covers his modest monthly expenses with room to spare, and his separate retirement savings exist purely as a bonus layer he could draw from freely without any risk at all. He has, in four years of retirement, withdrawn from that separate account exactly twice — once for a genuine emergency, a roof repair, and once, reluctantly, for a hearing aid his wife had been asking him to get for over a year. He describes the account, when asked, as money he's "not really touching," a phrase that treats an account built explicitly to be spent as though it were a museum piece, present but somehow off-limits, despite there being no plan, no advisor, and no math anywhere suggesting it should be.

What's actually happening

Start with what all three of these people actually know, because it matters enormously that their behavior isn't explained by ignorance. The engineer understands reservoirs professionally, at an expert level, and still can't apply that understanding to his own account. The teacher ran her own numbers and still flinches at an empty payday that was never going to arrive. Neither of them is confused about the facts. What's misfiring is not their arithmetic. It's a much older, much less conscious system — the one that spent thirty or forty years learning a single rule about money, and that rule was never about arithmetic at all.

For the entire span of a working life, the reservoir only fills. Contribution after contribution, paycheck after paycheck, arrives on a schedule, and the account grows, on the whole, across the decades, even through the inevitable dips along the way. A saver's nervous system, given that many years of consistent input, comes to treat "the account is fed regularly" as a stable, background fact about the world — not something anyone consciously thinks about, any more than anyone consciously thinks about gravity, but something the mind quietly builds an entire structure of confidence on top of. Every dollar spent during the working years is spent against the implicit backdrop of more arriving behind it. That backdrop is what makes spending during a working life feel, for most people, relatively uncomplicated. It isn't recklessness. It's a genuinely accurate read of the actual situation: more is, in fact, coming.

Retirement removes the backdrop entirely, on a specific and identifiable date, and it does so more completely than almost any other financial transition a person goes through in an ordinary life. This is worth sitting with, because it's easy to underestimate how total the shift actually is. A job loss during the working years is frightening, but it carries with it the implicit expectation of another job — the backdrop is disrupted, not permanently removed. A slow year in a business is stressful, but next year is still, in principle, available to be better. Retirement, for the vast majority of people, is different in kind, not just degree: the income source is not expected to return. There is no next paycheck coming, not next month, not next year, not ever again, in the specific form it arrived in for decades. The account that used to be fed is now, for the remainder of the saver's life, only drawn from. The direction has reversed, completely and permanently, and the nervous system that spent decades calibrating itself to one direction does not update to the new direction automatically, on schedule, just because a retirement party happened and a plaque got handed out.

This is where the mismatch between the life-cycle hypothesis described in this book's introduction and actual, observed retiree behavior becomes something you can feel rather than just something economists measure in aggregate data. Franco Modigliani's model, developed with Richard Brumberg in the 1950s, treats saving and spending as two phases of a single smooth, rational plan — save during the years of high income, spend down steadily during the years of low or no income, arrive near zero close to the end of life. What the model doesn't account for, because it's a model of rational allocation rather than a model of psychology, is that saving and spending aren't just two phases of the same plan to the person living through them. They're two entirely different behaviors, governed by two different systems, reinforced by decades of entirely different practice. Nobody spends thirty years training a muscle for release. The muscle trained for accumulation, exclusively, for as long as the saver was working — and asking it to suddenly perform the opposite motion, competently, on the strength of one meeting with a financial planner, is asking more of it than a single meeting can realistically deliver.

It's worth pausing, too, on why the direction of this reversal matters so much more than its size. A retiree drawing down a large account by a small percentage each year is, in absolute terms, making a far smaller change to their daily life than they made at almost any point during their working years, when a single job change, a single large purchase, or a single market swing could move their finances by a comparable amount without triggering anything like this level of distress. What's different isn't the magnitude. It's that every one of those working-years changes happened inside a system still oriented toward growth, where a dip was understood, correctly, as temporary. The retirement dip is not temporary, and the mind seems to register that distinction long before it can articulate it, treating even a genuinely small, well-planned decrease as evidence of something structurally wrong, simply because "structurally wrong" is the only category the mind has ever needed for a persistent decline before now.

There's a second, closely related mechanism worth calling out here, because it explains something the life-cycle gap alone doesn't fully account for: why the discomfort attaches specifically to withdrawal, rather than simply to a lower income in general. Daniel Kahneman and Amos Tversky's prospect theory, developed across the 1970s and formalized in their landmark 1979 paper, established that losses are experienced roughly twice as intensely as equivalently sized gains, measured against whatever a person currently treats as their reference point. For someone who spent decades watching an account rise, the account's own growing balance became, itself, the reference point — not a specific dollar figure, but the felt sense of "the number that's supposed to keep being at least this large, ideally larger." Every withdrawal in retirement moves the balance below whatever that felt reference point currently is, and prospect theory predicts, accurately, that this registers as a loss — a real, psychologically weighted loss, not a neutral bookkeeping event — regardless of whether the underlying plan considers the withdrawal completely safe. The financial planner's report can say, correctly, that the withdrawal is sustainable for thirty years. The part of the mind processing the withdrawal in the moment isn't consulting the report. It's registering a number that just got smaller than it was yesterday, and treating that, the way it would treat any loss, as something to be minimized rather than repeated.

It's worth being precise about what makes this loss-aversion response specific to retirement withdrawals rather than simply a general feature of how people relate to spending. During the working years, a large purchase also lowers an account balance temporarily — but it does so against a backdrop where the balance is expected to recover on the next payday, which blunts the loss signal considerably; a temporary dip that's known to be temporary registers very differently than a dip with no scheduled recovery behind it. In retirement, there is no scheduled recovery. Every withdrawal is, structurally, a permanent reduction against a pool that isn't being refilled the way it used to be, even when the underlying math accounts for exactly this pattern of drawdown and still comes out fine. The loss aversion isn't wrong about the direction of the change —

the number really is smaller after a withdrawal than before it. It's wrong about the significance of that change, treating a planned, sustainable, expected decrease as if it carried the same weight as an unplanned, threatening one.

The postal supervisor's version of this reflex is worth pausing on separately, because it shows the mechanism operating in its purest, least complicated form — no market volatility to point to, no genuine risk to cite, just a pension that already covers everything and a second account treated as though touching it required a permission slip nobody has ever actually required of him. What's notable is that he can articulate, clearly and without prompting, exactly why the account is safe to draw from. He simply hasn't drawn from it, because the mechanism this chapter describes doesn't require confusion to operate. It only requires an old rule — money in this account only grows — to still be running underneath a life that has, in every measurable way, already moved past the season that rule was built for. The hearing aid he delayed for over a year is the clearest evidence available that the rule, not the risk, was doing the deciding.

How to tell the difference. Not every hesitation before a withdrawal is this reflex, and it's worth being rigorous about that before assuming every moment of caution is a psychological problem to be solved. A retiree who pauses before an unusually large, one-time purchase to double-check it against their actual plan is doing exactly what a careful person should do — that pause is due diligence, not reflex. The reflex this chapter describes has a different signature: it shows up on ordinary, previously-verified, plan-approved withdrawals — the same monthly transfer a professional has already confirmed is safe, repeated month after month, each one still accompanied by the same private hesitation as the first, with no new information arriving each time to justify fresh doubt. If the hesitation fades once the numbers are checked and confirmed, that's healthy caution doing its job. If the hesitation returns, at full strength, every single time, on a transfer that's already been checked and confirmed a dozen times before, that's the reservoir defending an old rule rather than genuinely evaluating a new decision.

What it costs you

The most direct cost is the one already implied throughout this chapter: money that could have funded a fuller life instead sits unused, accumulating not toward any purpose but simply because releasing it feels wrong in a way no spreadsheet can talk a person out of. The engineer's eleven-day delay on that first plan-approved transfer isn't, by itself, expensive. But multiplied across the many transfers that follow it, month after month, year after year, a retiree who systematically underspends a well-supported plan by even a modest margin can leave behind, at the end of a life, a genuinely large sum of unused capacity — capacity that could have paid for a grandchild's wedding attended in person rather than watched over video, a hip repaired years earlier than it eventually was, a decade of winters spent somewhere warm instead of somewhere merely tolerable. None of that comes back. Unlike money, time spent underliving a well-funded retirement doesn't compound in reverse; a year of unnecessary caution at seventy-two isn't recoverable at eighty-nine, even with the exact same account balance sitting there, technically available the whole time.

There's a second cost, quieter and in some ways more corrosive, worth pointing out specifically: the erosion of trust between the retiree and their own plan. Every time the reflex overrides a decision the plan has already verified as safe, it reinforces a specific and damaging belief — that the plan can't actually be trusted, that the professional advice was somehow wrong even though nothing about the numbers has changed, that the only truly safe amount to spend is less than whatever the math says, indefinitely, with no floor. This isn't a one-time cost. It compounds the same way the loss-aversion signal compounds, each avoided withdrawal teaching the system that avoidance was the correct response, making the next withdrawal harder rather than easier, until a retiree who started retirement with a completely sound plan can find themselves, a decade in, unable to spend at even the conservative end of what that plan supports — not because the plan changed, but because the reflex got stronger with every repetition it was allowed to win.

There's a third cost specific to the teacher's version of this pattern, worth noting directly because it shows how the reflex reaches beyond spending decisions into the quality of everyday life. Her weekly tightening isn't tied to any specific purchase she's avoiding. It's a generalized contraction — a smaller grocery bill, a skipped coffee with a friend, a hesitation before a modest purchase that has nothing to do with her actual capacity to afford it — repeated across every week of a retirement that could, by her own verified numbers, be considerably more comfortable than the one she's actually living. This is the reflex operating at its most invisible and most costly: not as a single dramatic refusal, but as a low, constant tax on an entire life, paid in small increments too minor to individually notice, adding up, across years, to a retirement meaningfully smaller than the one she actually earned.

The postal supervisor's version carries its own specific cost, worth naming precisely because it looks, from the outside, like almost nothing happened. A missed hearing aid for a year is not a financial catastrophe by any measure, and it's tempting to read his story as low-stakes, even mildly amusing. But a year of strained conversations, of his wife repeating herself, of both of them quietly adjusting how they talk to each other around a problem that had an easy, fully funded solution sitting untouched the entire time, is not a small cost to the two people actually living inside it. The reflex doesn't need a dramatic dollar figure to do real damage. It only needs an ordinary year, repeated, in a marriage that could have been a little easier the whole time.

The overrides

Separate the account's two jobs, explicitly, in writing. For decades, the account had exactly one job: grow. It now has a second job it was never explicitly told about: fund your life. Write this down, literally, somewhere you'll see it — "this account's job is now to be spent, not just to grow" — because the old job doesn't quietly retire just because a new one has technically begun. Naming the second job in plain language, repeatedly, is the first step toward giving it equal standing against thirty years of practice defending the first one.

Reframe the withdrawal as the reservoir doing its designed job, not failing at it. The engineer's professional knowledge — that a reservoir which only fills and never releases is a flood risk, not a success — is available to him the moment he's willing to apply it to his own account instead of only to the systems he built for other people. Every retiree carries some version of this same knowledge somewhere in their life, some domain where they already understand that a system built for both accumulation and release only functions correctly when it does both. Find your own version of that knowledge, wherever it lives in your working life, and deliberately import it into the account you're now afraid to draw from.

The Move: automate the withdrawal the exact same way you automated the contribution. For decades, the deposit into this account happened without a decision — it was automatic, scheduled, removed from the need for willpower entirely, which is precisely why it was so reliably successful for so long. The withdrawal deserves the identical structure. If a specific, verified, plan-approved amount is set to transfer automatically, on a fixed schedule, with no monthly re-decision required, the reflex loses its usual opening — because the reflex needs a moment of active choice to intervene in, and a fully automated transfer, set up once and left alone, never offers it one.

Run the numbers with someone else present, every time the hesitation returns. The reflex thrives in private reconsideration — the quiet, solitary moment of staring at a screen and deciding, alone, that this time feels different even though nothing has actually changed. Bringing a spouse, a trusted friend, or the advisor who built the plan into that specific moment, even briefly, breaks the isolation the reflex depends on. Saying the hesitation out loud to another person, and hearing your own plan reflected back to you by someone not currently caught in the loss-aversion response, is often enough to interrupt it.

Track what the withdrawal actually funded, not just what it removed from the balance. The reflex measures cost almost exclusively in terms of the balance getting smaller. It rarely measures what the withdrawal purchased in return — the flight taken, the repair completed, the gift given, the month of genuine ease. Keeping a simple, ongoing record of what each withdrawal actually bought, reviewed alongside the balance rather than instead of it, gives the loss-aversion system a competing signal to weigh against the one it's currently weighing alone.

Practice on the smallest possible withdrawal first, deliberately, before the larger ones. The postal supervisor's two withdrawals in four years were both forced by circumstance — a roof, a hearing aid — never chosen. A deliberate, low-stakes practice withdrawal, made on no urgent occasion at all, for something genuinely minor, gives the nervous system a low-risk repetition to build confidence from, rather than only ever encountering the account in the high-stakes moments an emergency happens to create. Confidence built on a five-dollar decision transfers, eventually, to a five-hundred-dollar one.

The engineer opens the laptop on day twelve, not because the discomfort has resolved — it hasn't, not fully, not yet — but because his wife asks him, directly, why an account both of them agreed, in writing, with a professional present, could support this exact transfer is still sitting untouched. He doesn't have a good answer. He clicks confirm. Nothing happens that he didn't expect to happen: the balance drops by the planned amount, and the world continues exactly as it was the day before, except that the money is now doing something instead of nothing. He tells his wife, later, that it felt like turning a valve he'd spent forty years teaching other people how to build and had never, until that moment, actually turned himself.

The Rule to Remember: the account was never built to only fill. It was built to fill and then release — and the release is not the reservoir failing at its job. It's the reservoir finally doing the second half of it.

Chapter 2 — The Balance That Only Falls

A retired accountant, three years into retirement, checks his portfolio balance most mornings before he's finished his coffee, the way he's checked it most mornings for the past thirty years. For three decades, the ritual had a specific emotional shape: some mornings the number was up, some mornings it was down, and over any long enough stretch, the direction that actually mattered — the multi-year trend — was reliably, comfortably up. He'd learned, the way anyone who watches markets for decades learns, not to react much to any single day. Retirement changed the ritual without changing the behavior. Now, most months, the number is down from the month before — not dramatically, not dangerously, exactly as his withdrawal plan predicted it would be, a slow, planned, entirely sustainable decline toward a target that still leaves him comfortable at ninety-five. But his morning coffee ritual hasn't updated to the new context. Every down month still registers, in his chest, as the identical sensation a down month registered during his working years — except that during his working years, the down months were noise around an upward trend. Now the down months are the trend, and no part of him has caught up to the fact that this particular kind of down is supposed to be happening.

A retired social worker describes a related but distinct version of the same discomfort to her sister over the phone. She isn't checking her balance obsessively — if anything, she's started avoiding her retirement account statement almost entirely, letting three or four months pass unopened. When her sister asks why, she says, almost embarrassed, that she already knows what it's going to say — smaller than last time — and she'd rather not watch it happen in real time. She isn't in any danger. Her withdrawal rate is conservative, verified twice by a fee-only planner she trusts. But she has started organizing a meaningful part of her emotional life around simply not looking, the way a person avoids a scale during a period they already suspect isn't going well, even when the underlying reality is, in her case, completely fine.

A retired veterinarian offers a third variation, one that shows the same underlying discomfort expressing itself as compulsive recalculation rather than either daily checking or avoidance. She doesn't look at her account balance more than her advisor recommends, and she doesn't avoid it either. What she does instead is re-run her own withdrawal math, by hand, on a legal pad, roughly once a week — the same calculation her advisor already performs professionally, cross-checked twice a year, with tools considerably more sophisticated than a legal pad and a calculator. Her numbers always come out close to her advisor's. She runs them again anyway, the following week, and the week after that, describing the habit to her husband as "just making sure," a phrase that, said once, sounds like ordinary diligence, and said every week for three years starts to sound like something closer to a ritual performed to manage a discomfort the numbers themselves were never actually going to resolve.

What's actually happening

All three of these responses — the accountant's daily flinch, the social worker's avoidance, and the veterinarian's compulsive recalculation — are downstream of the same asymmetry, and it's worth being precise about what that asymmetry actually is, because it isn't simply "loss aversion" in the generic sense this library has already introduced elsewhere. It's a specific version of loss aversion that applies to a fixed, non-replenishing pool, and it behaves differently from the loss aversion that governs ordinary investment behavior during the working years.

During the working years, loss aversion mostly shows up around market volatility — the discomfort of watching a portfolio's value drop during a downturn, even though the money hasn't actually been spent or lost in any permanent sense, just temporarily marked down on paper. That version of loss aversion, well documented by Kahneman and Tversky's prospect theory, is uncomfortable but usually resolves itself: markets that fall, over long enough horizons, have historically recovered, and a working saver has time, and future contributions, working in their favor while they wait it out. Retirement withdrawal loss aversion is a different animal, because the decline it's reacting to isn't a temporary paper loss waiting to recover — it's a real, planned, permanent reduction, the account genuinely getting smaller by design, with no future paycheck arriving to offset it. The accountant's morning flinch and the social worker's avoidance are both, in their own way, entirely accurate readings of a genuinely new fact: for the first time in either of their adult lives, "the balance went down" is not a temporary blip. It's the plan working correctly. Their nervous systems simply never learned to feel the difference between a decline that's a problem and a decline that's the point.

This connects to something economists specifically studying retirement have documented under the name of the annuity puzzle — a well-established finding, examined across decades of research by economists including Jeffrey Brown, that most retirees, given the option, decline to convert a portion of their savings into an annuity, a financial instrument that trades a lump sum for a guaranteed stream of income for life, even when the underlying math often favors the trade for a meaningful share of retirees. Economists have proposed several explanations for the puzzle, but one of the most consistently supported is exactly the mechanism this chapter describes: retirees experience the ongoing sight of a shrinking account balance as more distressing than the underlying financial reality warrants, and some part of that distress persists even for retirees who intellectually understand that an annuitized income stream would functionally solve the exact discomfort they're experiencing — because giving up the lump sum, converting a large, visible, falling number into a smaller, stable, monthly one, still requires confronting the falling-balance discomfort directly, once, at the moment of conversion, and the reflex would rather avoid that single confrontation than accept the long-term relief on the other side of it. This book takes no position on whether any individual reader should or shouldn't consider an annuity — that's a conversation for a licensed financial professional working from actual numbers, not a psychology book. What matters for this chapter is what the puzzle reveals about the underlying reflex: even when a financial instrument exists specifically to solve the falling-balance discomfort, many retirees avoid that solution because engaging with it means looking directly at the falling balance one more time, and the avoidance instinct is often stronger than the relief on offer.

There's a related concept worth introducing here, because it explains why avoidance — the social worker's unopened statements — can feel, in the moment, like the more comfortable choice, even though it typically makes the underlying discomfort worse over time rather than better. Behavioral researchers have documented a pattern sometimes called the ostrich effect — the tendency to avoid checking on financial information specifically when that information is expected to be unwelcome, even when regular monitoring would, on average, lead to better decisions. The term is informal rather than the name of a single foundational study, but the underlying pattern — selective attention to financial information, calibrated to whether the news is likely to be good or bad — has been documented across multiple lines of behavioral finance research. It maps precisely onto the social worker's unopened envelopes. She isn't avoiding the statement because she doesn't care about her finances; she's avoided it precisely because she cares, and because some part of her has pre-decided that "smaller than last time" is inherently bad news, rather than the expected and entirely sustainable shape of a well-run decumulation plan. The avoidance doesn't protect her from anything real. It just delays the moment she has to feel the discomfort, and delayed discomfort, unlike delayed spending, doesn't compound in her favor.

The veterinarian's compulsive recalculation looks, on the surface, like the opposite response to the social worker's avoidance — engagement rather than retreat — but it's worth sitting with why it belongs to the same family rather than a genuinely different one. Repeatedly re-verifying information that's already been verified is a well-documented feature of anxiety more broadly, sometimes described in the clinical literature as reassurance-seeking: a behavior that produces short-term relief immediately after it's performed, which is exactly what makes it so persistent, while doing nothing to reduce the underlying uncertainty driving it, because the uncertainty was never really about the accuracy of the number in the first place. Her advisor's calculation and her own legal-pad calculation could not possibly be more aligned, and the alignment still isn't what settles her, because what she's actually managing, week after week, isn't a math problem. It's the identical falling-balance discomfort the accountant and the social worker are managing through their own, different channels — hers simply expresses itself as a compulsion to keep re-confirming a fact she has already, correctly, confirmed many times before.

There's a further layer worth adding, because it explains why the discomfort of a falling balance doesn't stay fixed at one intensity across a retirement but tends to sharpen at certain points and ease at others. Behavioral economists working in the tradition of reference-dependent preferences — building on Kahneman and Tversky's original framework — have documented that the reference point itself, the number a person measures gains and losses against, is not fixed. It drifts, gradually, to match whatever level a person has grown accustomed to over a sustained period. This has a specific and somewhat counterintuitive implication for retirement: the sharpest discomfort tends to arrive not at the largest withdrawal, but at the first one, and again at any withdrawal that breaks a recently settled pattern, because the reference point hasn't yet drifted to accommodate the new, lower normal. The accountant's daily flinch was, by his own account, considerably more intense in his first year of retirement than in his third — not because the withdrawals became smaller, but because his reference point had, by year three, quietly recalibrated to include the fact of ongoing decline as the new baseline rather than a repeated violation of an old one.

How to tell the difference. A balance that's falling because of genuine overspending against a plan is a real problem, and no amount of psychological reframing should talk you out of noticing it. The distinguishing question is whether the rate of decline matches what a verified plan predicted, or whether it's meaningfully outpacing it. If your most recent professional review confirmed the current trajectory is sustainable for your full projected lifespan, a falling balance within that range is the plan working as designed — a fact, not a warning. If you haven't had that trajectory verified recently, or if the decline is visibly steeper than what was projected, that's not this chapter's reflex. That's a legitimate signal worth taking to whoever built your plan, promptly and without embarrassment.

What it costs you

The accountant's daily check, repeated across a retirement that could last twenty or thirty years, adds up to an extraordinary quantity of small, unnecessary distress — a flinch experienced most mornings, for years, in response to something his own verified plan has already told him is not a problem. That distress doesn't stay contained to the moment of checking. It bleeds outward into decisions across the rest of his day, making him quicker to decline a lunch invitation, slower to book the trip he and his wife have discussed for years, more likely to describe himself, when asked, as "watching things carefully right now" even in years when nothing about his finances actually calls for extra watching. A morning ritual meant to provide reassurance has become, instead, a daily reinforcement of exactly the fear it was originally meant to manage.

The social worker's avoidance carries a different and in some ways riskier cost, because avoidance, unlike hypervigilance, removes the very information a person would need to notice if something genuinely did go wrong. A retiree who has trained themselves not to look at their statements is well-positioned to miss the actual warning signs — a withdrawal rate that's crept up faster than planned, an unexpected expense that's meaningfully changed the trajectory — precisely because the habit of not looking was built to manage a false alarm and doesn't know how to distinguish a false alarm from a real one. The irony is exact: the coping mechanism built to avoid unnecessary worry is the same mechanism that would delay catching necessary worry, should it ever actually arrive.

There's a shared cost worth saying outright across all three versions of this pattern: the falling balance, treated as an ongoing source of dread rather than a neutral, expected feature of a well-run retirement, quietly recolors the entire experience of having saved successfully. All three of these people did the hard work. All three built accounts capable of funding decades of comfortable life. And all three are experiencing some real portion of those decades — the very years the saving was for — under a low, persistent cloud of financial anxiety that their own numbers don't support. The plan worked. The felt experience of living inside it hasn't caught up, and every year that gap persists is a year of a well-earned retirement spent, at least in part, somewhere other than where the numbers actually place them.

The veterinarian's cost is specific to the time itself: hours, across three years, spent re-deriving a number that never once meaningfully changed from her advisor's professional figure. Those hours weren't spent worrying about something real. They were spent performing a ritual that felt, in the moment, like productive caution, and that time — an evening a week, most weeks, for three years — is time that could have gone toward almost anything else her verified plan already supports without a second look.

The overrides

Reframe the check-in, not the frequency. For the accountant, the problem isn't checking daily — for some people, regular monitoring is genuinely reassuring, and there's no rule that says frequency itself is the issue. The problem is what he's checking for. Before opening the account each morning, name explicitly what a "normal" range looks like this month, according to the verified plan — a specific number or narrow range, written down in advance — so that the daily check becomes a comparison against an expected target rather than an open-ended search for reassurance that a falling number can never actually provide.

Schedule the review instead of avoiding it, and bring backup. For the social worker's pattern, the fix isn't forcing daily exposure — that would likely just intensify the avoidance.

It's converting an unpredictable, dreaded event into a scheduled, bounded one: a specific day each quarter, ideally with the advisor or a trusted person present, to review the statement together rather than alone. A scheduled, accompanied review removes both the uncertainty of not knowing when the dreaded moment will strike and the isolation of facing it without anyone else's perspective in the room.

The Move: replace the balance with the runway. A single balance number, viewed in isolation, tells you almost nothing about whether decline is a problem — it just tells you the account is smaller than it was, which loss aversion will always register as bad news regardless of context. A runway figure — "at the current spending rate, this plan is verified to last until age ninety-four" — gives the same underlying information a genuinely different emotional shape, because a runway that's comfortably longer than your actual life expectancy reads as safety, not decline, even while the raw balance underneath it continues, correctly, to fall. Ask your advisor for this figure specifically, in these terms, and check that instead of the balance when the urge to check arises.

Separate volatility from decumulation on your statement, visually, if your provider allows it. Part of what makes the falling balance so viscerally uncomfortable is that ordinary month-to-month market volatility and planned, intentional withdrawal get blended into a single number, making it impossible to tell, at a glance, how much of any given month's decline was the market and how much was simply the plan working as designed. Where your provider offers it, separate these two components — even a simple side-by-side note, "market movement this month" versus "planned withdrawal this month" — gives the loss-aversion system a clearer, less alarming picture than one blended number ever can.

Name the specific number the reference point is currently defending. Because the reference point drifts rather than staying fixed, it helps to make it explicit rather than leaving it to operate silently in the background. Ask directly: what specific balance, right now, feels like "normal" — the number that would need to be crossed downward before real alarm feels warranted. Writing that number down, and comparing it honestly to what the verified plan actually requires as a floor, often reveals a private, unexamined alarm threshold set considerably higher than any real danger point, simply because it drifted upward during a period of comfortable growth and was never deliberately reset for the different shape of a retirement account.

Give the recalculation compulsion a hard stop, in writing, agreed to in advance. For a pattern like the veterinarian's, the fix isn't refusing to ever double-check the math — occasional verification is reasonable. It's setting an explicit limit, decided while calm and not currently mid-compulsion: math gets reviewed at the scheduled semi-annual meeting, and not in between, with a specific, pre-agreed response ready for the urge to recalculate anyway — a walk, a phone call to a friend, anything that isn't the legal pad. The goal isn't eliminating the anxiety in one attempt. It's breaking the specific link between the anxious feeling and the compulsive recalculation that currently, temporarily, soothes it.

Half a year into deliberately practicing the runway reframe, the accountant notices something he mentions almost in passing to his wife: he's stopped opening the account first thing every morning. Not because he's forced himself to stop, and not because he's stopped caring. He simply reaches for it less, because the number he's actually tracking now — a runway comfortably past ninety-four — doesn't move enough, month to month, to produce the same daily pull the raw balance used to. The falling number is still falling, exactly as planned. It's just stopped feeling, each morning, like news.

The veterinarian, after three months of holding to the agreed limit, describes the first few weeks as genuinely uncomfortable — the urge to pull out the legal pad arrived on schedule, most weeks, exactly as strong as before. What changed was that she had somewhere specific to put the urge instead of acting on it: a short walk, most times, sometimes a call to her sister instead. By the third month, she tells her husband, the urge itself had started arriving less often, not because the underlying math ever changed, but because a compulsion given nowhere to land eventually, gradually, stops asking as loudly.

The Rule to Remember: a balance that falls on schedule isn't losing. It's spending — and spending, for the first time in your working life, was always supposed to be the whole

point of the number you spent decades building.

Chapter 3 — The Budget That Never Retires

A retired airline pilot spends the first eighteen months of retirement running his household budget with the exact same discipline he ran preflight checklists for thirty-one years — a discipline that served him and every passenger who ever boarded one of his flights extremely well, and that he has never once questioned as a general approach to life. What's changed is what the checklist is now checking for. During his working years, the budget's job was to make sure spending didn't outpace an income that was, itself, reliably growing. Now, eighteen months into a retirement his advisor has confirmed, twice, in writing, can support a specific and fairly generous monthly spending target, his budget still runs on the tighter, working-years number — the one calibrated to a salary that no longer exists, in a category of caution that made complete sense when he was still earning and makes considerably less sense now. He doesn't consciously decide to ignore the advisor's higher number. He simply keeps running the old checklist, because the old checklist has never once, in thirty-one years, let him down, and switching to a new one feels, in some hard-to-articulate way, like abandoning the exact discipline that got him here safely.

A retired nurse who spent thirty-four years on a hospital floor describes a related pattern with a specific, almost ritualistic edge to it. Every purchase over a hundred dollars still gets run through a mental version of triage — the same instinct she used for decades to sort incoming patients by urgency, now redirected entirely onto her own spending. Is this necessary. Can it wait. Is there a version that costs less. She applies this triage to purchases her own verified retirement plan could easily absorb without noticing — a plane ticket to visit her son, a set of new tires before the old ones are dangerously worn but well past their recommended life, a massage her physical therapist has actually recommended for a chronic shoulder issue from decades of patient transfers. None of these purchases threaten her financial security in any way her advisor has flagged. All of them get triaged, delayed, or downgraded anyway, because the triage instinct doesn't check the account balance before it runs. It just runs, on every purchase, the way it ran on every patient for three and a half decades.

A retired office manager offers a third version of the same pattern, distinct enough to be worth including on its own. For twenty-two years, she managed a mid-sized firm's operating budget with a specific monthly ritual: closing out every category on the last business day of the month, reconciling every dollar, flagging anything over budget for review. In retirement, with no firm and no operating budget left to manage, she has kept the exact ritual running against her own household finances — a full, formal, end-of-month reconciliation, every category flagged and reviewed, applied to a retirement budget her advisor has confirmed could run considerably looser without any risk at all. She isn't distressed by the ritual; if anything, she describes it as satisfying, a familiar rhythm she genuinely enjoys. What she hasn't noticed is that the ritual's underlying strictness — treating any category that runs over as a problem requiring correction — has quietly imported thirty years of institutional budget discipline into a household account that was never supposed to be managed with an institution's tolerance for overage.

What's actually happening

What all three of these patterns share is a specific kind of persistence — not the general habit of being financially careful, which most successful savers carry throughout their lives in some form, but the very particular persistence of a system that was calibrated under one set of conditions and never received the update that the conditions changed. This is worth distinguishing clearly from ordinary budgeting discipline, because the pilot and the nurse would both, correctly, describe themselves as disciplined people, and this chapter isn't arguing that discipline itself is the problem. The problem is more specific: the discipline is still defending a target that hasn't been recalibrated to match a plan that has, in fact, already changed.

Behavioral economics has a well-established name for a closely related pattern, developed by the economist Richard Thaler working with Hersh Shefrin in their 1981 paper on self-control, later expanded across Thaler's broader body of work on what he termed mental accounting. Mental accounting describes the tendency people have to treat money as belonging to separate, non-interchangeable categories in their minds — a bonus treated differently than a paycheck, a birthday gift treated differently than earned income, even though a dollar is, in strict economic terms, identical no matter which mental account it's assigned to. Applied to retirement budgeting, mental accounting explains something specific and important: the pilot's mind never actually reassigned his "working budget" into a new "retirement budget" category. It simply kept running the old category, unaware that the underlying conditions justifying that category's specific limits had changed, because mental accounts, once formed, are remarkably sticky — they don't automatically dissolve or update just because the external facts that originally justified them have shifted. Someone has to deliberately close the old account and open a new one, and that deliberate act, simple as it sounds, is precisely the step most retirees never consciously take.

There's a second mechanism worth layering on top of the mental-accounting explanation, because it explains why the old budget doesn't just persist passively but actively resists being loosened even when the new, higher number has been clearly presented. Status quo bias — documented rigorously by the economists William Samuelson and Richard Zeckhauser in their 1988 paper on decision-making — describes a durable, well-replicated preference for the current state of affairs, independent of whether a change would objectively improve a person's position. The pilot's old budget isn't just a leftover mental account; it's also, simply, the current state of affairs, the default his household has run on for years, and defaults carry their own gravitational pull entirely apart from whether they're still the correct number. Loosening the budget requires actively overriding a default that's felt correct, and been correct, for decades — which is a meaningfully harder psychological task than simply following a default that's never once been questioned.

It's worth being specific about why the nurse's triage instinct in particular is so hard to retire, because it points to something the pilot's version of this chapter doesn't fully capture on its own. Her triage habit wasn't built around a household budget at all — it was built around a professional skill honed under genuine scarcity, where hospital resources, staff time, and attention really were finite and really did need rationing, and where the cost of miscalibrating that rationing, in her actual working life, could be measured in patient outcomes. That kind of high-stakes training doesn't simply switch off because the context changed from a hospital floor to a personal checking account with ample funds. The skill generalized, the way well-trained professional instincts often do, well beyond the specific domain it was built for — which made her an excellent nurse for thirty-four years, and which now makes her an unnecessarily austere retiree in a life that, by her own verified numbers, doesn't require rationing at all.

The office manager's version adds a further wrinkle worth flagging precisely, because unlike the pilot's calibration problem or the nurse's scarcity training, her old system was never actually built around scarcity at all — it was built around institutional accountability, a framework designed to answer to other people about other people's money. A firm's operating budget gets reconciled strictly because someone eventually has to explain any overage to a board, an owner, an auditor. A household retirement budget answers to no one but the two people living inside it, and a plan that's already been verified to comfortably support some months running over is not the same category of problem an institutional budget variance would be. The office manager isn't managing her own scarcity or another person's crisis. She's managing an accountability structure that has no actual audience left to answer to, and running it anyway, out of thirty years of habit, on a household that was never the intended subject of that particular discipline.

There's a useful, practical concept worth introducing here from a different corner of psychology, because it points directly toward this chapter's most effective override rather than simply describing the problem further. The psychologist Peter Gollwitzer's research on implementation intentions, developed across numerous studies since the mid-1990s, found that simply forming a general intention — "I will spend more" — is a considerably weaker predictor of actual behavior change than forming a specific, if-then plan tied to a concrete trigger: "when the quarterly review happens, I will increase the transfer to the verified amount." Gollwitzer's research found that this kind of specific, pre-committed linkage between a cue and an action substantially outperforms general intentions across a wide range of behaviors, precisely because it removes the need for in-the-moment willpower, replacing an open-ended resolution with an automatic response to a fixed trigger. Both the pilot's and the nurse's old habits already function as involuntary implementation intentions of exactly this kind — running automatically, tied to a trigger, requiring no willpower at all. The fix isn't inventing a new psychological skill neither of them has. It's redirecting a skill they've already mastered, at full strength, toward a different, updated trigger and outcome.

How to tell the difference. A retiree genuinely operating on a tight, real budget — one where the numbers actually require careful tracking of every purchase — is not the subject of this chapter, and nothing here should talk that retiree into spending beyond what their real plan supports. The reflex this chapter describes has a specific, checkable signature: a budget that has been explicitly, formally revised upward by a verified plan, and that the retiree's actual month-to-month spending has failed to move toward, months or years after the revision. If your monthly spending roughly matches your most recently verified plan, your budget is doing its job correctly, whatever its size. If your verified plan says one number and your actual spending has stayed anchored to a meaningfully smaller one, month after month, with no real change in circumstance to explain the gap, that's this chapter's reflex, not prudent budgeting.

What it costs you

The most direct cost is the gap itself, compounding across every month it's allowed to persist: the difference between what a verified plan says is safely available and what actually gets spent, multiplied across the years of a retirement that, for most successful savers, runs considerably longer than the eighteen months the pilot has so far lived through it. That gap doesn't accumulate as savings in any meaningful sense — the money isn't being redirected toward some other worthwhile goal. It simply sits, unused, funding nothing, while the specific years capable of enjoying it pass by underneath a budget calibrated for a working life that's already over.

There's a subtler cost specific to the rigidity of an unrevised budget category, worth stating plainly on its own: the erosion, over time, of a retiree's confidence in their own judgment about money. Every time the old budget number wins against the new, verified one, it reinforces a quiet, false lesson — that the old number was somehow more real than the new one, that the professional recalibration was the anomaly and the working-years discipline was the true baseline. This isn't a neutral wash. It actively works against every future attempt at revision, because a person who has spent eighteen months privately concluding that their advisor's higher number "doesn't feel right" has built up eighteen months of evidence, entirely self-generated, for distrusting exactly the kind of professional guidance that could otherwise correct the pattern.

The nurse's version of this cost carries a specific and painful edge worth calling out directly: some of what gets triaged away isn't a luxury at all, but genuine, advisable self-care — the massage her own physical therapist recommended for a documented, decades-earned shoulder problem, the flight to see a son she doesn't see often enough. A rationing instinct built for genuine medical scarcity, applied inappropriately to a well-funded retirement, doesn't just delay minor comforts. It can delay the exact category of spending — health, connection, physical relief from decades of demanding work — that a retirement plan exists specifically to make possible, trading real, earned quality of life for a caution the numbers never actually required.

The office manager's cost is quieter but worth pointing out for what it does to the tone of an entire household, month after month: a reconciliation ritual that flags any overage as a problem requiring review, applied to a retirement that could comfortably absorb far more variance than that, tends to manufacture a low background tension around spending that has no actual financial basis. Her husband has learned, over the years since her retirement began, to brace slightly at the end of each month, anticipating a conversation about a grocery category that ran twenty dollars over — a conversation her own advisor would tell her, if asked directly, simply doesn't need to happen. The cost isn't the twenty dollars. It's a household tone calibrated to a scrutiny level neither of them actually needs anymore.

The overrides

Formally retire the old budget, in a specific, deliberate act. Mental accounts don't dissolve on their own; they have to be actively closed. Sit down, on a specific date, and write out the old, working-years budget explicitly — categories, numbers, limits — and then write, beside it, the new, verified retirement numbers, category by category. The act of writing both down side by side, deliberately, is what mental-accounting research suggests is required to actually close the old account rather than simply letting it keep running underneath the new one unacknowledged.

Give the old checklist a new, explicit job. The pilot's checklist discipline isn't the problem — it's a genuinely valuable skill, and this book has no interest in talking him out of it. The fix isn't abandoning the checklist; it's rewriting what it checks for. A retirement-specific checklist, built with the same rigor he brought to a preflight routine, but calibrated to the actual, verified retirement numbers rather than the old working-years ones, lets him keep the exact discipline he trusts while finally pointing it at the correct target.

The Move: revise the budget on a fixed schedule, out loud, with another person present, whether or not it feels necessary. A budget revision that only happens when a retiree feels ready for it will, for most people carrying this reflex, never actually happen — the reflex is precisely the thing preventing readiness from arriving on its own. Scheduling a mandatory, calendar-fixed review — every six months, with a spouse, an advisor, or a trusted friend present — removes the need to feel ready and replaces it with a standing appointment the reflex has no real hold over.

Give the checklist instinct a genuine second target, not just permission to relax. Neither the pilot's nor the nurse's discipline is going to simply switch off because a book told them the old target no longer applies — that instinct is too deeply trained, and too core to how each of them operates, to expect it to go quiet. A more realistic goal is redirection: hand the checklist instinct an actual, ongoing second job — auditing whether spending matches the verified plan, rather than whether spending stays below an old ceiling — so the discipline itself stays fully engaged, simply pointed, finally, at the correct question.

Rebuild the professional-skill transfer deliberately, in the other direction. The nurse's triage instinct generalized from her profession into her personal finances without her ever choosing that transfer; it can be redirected the same way, on purpose. Instead of applying triage logic to whether a purchase is necessary, apply it to whether her verified plan supports it — a different, and more accurate, urgency question entirely. "Is this within what my plan can absorb" is a triage question exactly as rigorous as the one she ran for three decades on a hospital floor. It's simply asking about the correct patient.

Rename the review from "reconciliation" to something that doesn't carry institutional weight. Language matters more than it seems like it should here. "Reconciling" a budget category implies a discrepancy requiring resolution; a household account genuinely doesn't need that framing once its verified plan already tolerates real variance. Simply renaming the monthly ritual — a "check-in" instead of a "reconciliation," a "look" instead of a "review" — can measurably soften the strict, corrective posture a thirty-year professional habit brings to a task that no longer requires it.

Build in a tolerance band, explicitly, the way a verified plan actually has one. The office manager's institutional habit treats any overage as a flag requiring review, but her actual retirement plan, like most well-built ones, already has real slack built into it — a range within which spending can vary month to month without threatening anything. Writing that tolerance band down explicitly, in the same document as the budget categories themselves, gives her reconciliation ritual an accurate stopping point: review anything outside the band, and treat anything inside it, correctly, as not a variance at all.

The nurse's first attempt at the redirected triage question comes with the shoulder massage her physical therapist recommended months earlier. She runs the new question instead of the old one — not "is this necessary," but "does my plan support this" — and the answer, checked against the actual numbers rather than against decades of scarcity training, is an easy yes. She books it the same afternoon, before the old instinct has time to reassert itself, and describes the appointment afterward, to her sister, as the first purchase in eighteen months that didn't come with an argument attached.

The office manager, at her advisor's suggestion, writes her tolerance band directly into the same notebook she's used for years to run her monthly reconciliation, right beside the categories themselves. The first month she lets a grocery overage sit unflagged inside the band, she reports feeling a small, specific itch to note it anyway — thirty years of institutional habit doesn't dissolve in a single month. She lets the itch pass without acting on it. By the following quarter, she tells her husband the end-of-month ritual finally feels like hers again, rather than a firm's, run for an audience that was never actually going to ask.

The Rule to Remember: the checklist that got you here safely is not the same checklist you need now — and running the wrong one with total discipline is still running the wrong one.

Chapter 4 — The Price Tag That Feels Like a Verdict

A retired machinist, two years into retirement, can authorize a property tax payment, a health insurance premium, and a new furnace without a flicker of hesitation — each one landing, in his mind, in a mental folder labeled something like "obligations," a category that has never once required deliberation because obligations, by definition, simply get paid. The same man spends four months circling a decision about whether to buy himself a decent set of woodworking tools, a hobby he's wanted to properly take up for over a decade and that his verified retirement plan can absorb without measurable impact. The furnace cost more than the tools would. He didn't hesitate on the furnace. The tools sit in a different mental folder entirely — something closer to "wants," and in his internal accounting, that folder operates under an entirely different, much stricter set of rules, rules that have nothing to do with what either category actually costs and everything to do with what each category is quietly labeled.

A retired travel agent, who spent twenty-six years booking other people's vacations, describes an almost identical split with a specific, ironic edge: she can approve a home repair, a medical copay, or a gift for a grandchild within minutes of the request arriving, but has not booked a single trip for herself in the two years since she retired, despite having spent her entire career telling clients, correctly, that travel while healthy and mobile is one of the most reliably valuable uses of retirement money there is. When her daughter asks why, directly, over dinner, she says the trip "isn't necessary right now" — a phrase she recognizes, even as she says it, as one she'd have gently pushed back on if a client had used it on her twenty years earlier. She knows the advice. She has simply never applied her own professional judgment to the account with her own name on it.

A retired court reporter offers a third example of the same split, notable for how clearly she can articulate the rule even while following it. She keeps, without any embarrassment, an actual informal list in her head — she'll recite it if asked — of purchases that "count" as acceptable without discussion: anything for her house, anything for her grandchildren, anything medically necessary. Everything else, including a subscription to a lecture series she's wanted for two years, a series her verified plan could fund a hundred times over without noticing, gets held in a kind of permanent pending status, neither approved nor declined, just never quite acted on. She knows the list is arbitrary. She built it herself, consciously, sometime in her forties, as a way of keeping spending disciplined during years when disciplined spending genuinely mattered. She has simply never revisited it since, the way a rule written for one set of circumstances can keep quietly governing behavior long after those circumstances changed.

What's actually happening

All three of these patterns are a specific, retirement-flavored expression of Richard Thaler's mental accounting, introduced in the previous chapter, but applied here to a different axis: not the old budget versus the new one, but the moral coding attached to different categories of spending regardless of what either category actually costs. Thaler's broader body of work on mental accounting, including his influential 1985 paper on the topic and subsequent research, documents how people build largely arbitrary internal categories for money and then apply wildly inconsistent rules across those categories — treating a windfall as more spendable than an identical sum earned through ordinary income, treating money already "spent" on a non-refundable ticket as a sunk cost that shouldn't influence future decisions even when it psychologically does. The categories this chapter is concerned with are "necessary" and "frivolous" — two labels that feel, to the person applying them, like objective descriptions of the purchase itself, when they're actually a subjective, largely inherited moral judgment that has almost nothing to do with dollar amount and everything to do with which category a given purchase happened to get sorted into, often decades earlier, based on rules absorbed long before either the machinist or the travel agent had any real financial agency of their own.

It's worth being precise about where this particular sorting rule tends to originate, because "necessary versus frivolous" isn't a neutral, universal split — it's calibrated by a specific cultural and generational inheritance around the moral weight of spending on obligations to others versus spending on oneself.

Many people who came of age with a strong ethic of duty, provision, and responsibility toward family absorbed, early and thoroughly, the belief that spending directed outward — toward a home, a family member, an institution, an obligation — carries an automatic legitimacy that spending directed inward, toward one's own pleasure or comfort, has to actively earn. This isn't irrational on its face; a genuine ethic of responsibility toward others is not, in itself, a problem this book is trying to talk anyone out of. What becomes a problem, specifically in retirement, is that this asymmetric legitimacy doesn't recalibrate once a person's plan has been verified to comfortably support both categories. The furnace stays in the effortless folder. The woodworking tools stay in the folder that requires four months of internal litigation, regardless of the fact that a professional has confirmed both categories fit easily within the same well-funded plan.

There's a related concept worth introducing here that sharpens why this particular asymmetry is so resistant to simple correction: the endowment effect, first formally demonstrated by Richard Thaler in his 1980 paper on consumer choice and expanded in subsequent experimental work, describes the finding that people consistently value something more once they own it than they would value the identical thing before owning it — a mug given to a participant in an experiment, for instance, gets priced by its new owner well above what an equally informed buyer would offer for it. Applied to retirement savings, a version of this effect helps explain why money framed as belonging to a specific external obligation — the mortgage, the grandchild's tuition, the family emergency fund — feels, once mentally assigned to that purpose, almost sacred in its legitimacy, defended without hesitation, while the identical sum of money framed only as "spending on myself" never received that same mental assignment of ownership-to-a-purpose, and so never picked up the endowment effect's protective legitimacy. The furnace was, in the machinist's mind, always going to be paid for the moment it broke, because a broken furnace has an obvious, externally-assigned purpose no one would argue with. The woodworking tools never received an equivalent assignment, because nobody handed him a bill for them the way the furnace company did — he would have had to assign that legitimacy to himself, on his own authority, and that turns out to be a meaningfully harder thing to do than simply paying a bill someone else generated.

The court reporter's list is worth examining for what it reveals about how these categories actually get built in the first place, because unlike the machinist's or the travel agent's more diffuse sense of what counts, hers was a conscious, deliberate rule, written by an earlier version of herself under real financial pressure decades ago. That earlier version had good reasons for the rule; discretionary spending genuinely did need to be restrained during the years the rule was built for. What she hasn't done is the second half of the work — retiring a rule once the conditions that justified it have changed, the same specific failure this book's earlier chapters have already traced in other forms. A category built deliberately, for real reasons, doesn't become less sticky than one absorbed passively; if anything, having built it herself gives it a kind of personal authority that makes it feel less like an outdated rule and more like a fact about her own character, which is precisely what makes it so much harder to simply set down.

It's worth noting directly, too, why this particular mislabeling survives contact with so much contrary evidence over the years, because both the machinist and the travel agent are intelligent people perfectly capable of noticing the inconsistency if they looked directly at it. Mental accounting, in Thaler's broader framework, isn't merely a set of categories — it's a set of categories that people are strongly motivated not to examine too closely, because the categories serve a real, if largely unconscious, function: they simplify an otherwise overwhelming number of individual spending decisions into a small number of fast, low-effort rules. Examining the rule closely enough to notice its inconsistency would require exactly the kind of deliberate, effortful reconsideration the category was built to avoid in the first place. This is part of why an outside observer so often spots the imbalance instantly, in a single glance, that the person living inside the pattern has managed not to notice for years. The categories are invisible from the inside precisely because their whole function is to prevent the kind of scrutiny that would reveal them.

How to tell the difference. Not every hesitation before a personal purchase reflects this reflex — some genuine wants really are worth deferring, and a retiree with real reasons to prioritize other categories of spending isn't automatically caught in the pattern this chapter describes. The distinguishing signature here is the size of the gap between how quickly a purchase gets approved when it's framed as an obligation to someone or something else, versus how much deliberation an equivalent or even smaller purchase requires when it's framed as being for the retiree alone. If both categories get roughly similar scrutiny relative to their actual cost, that's simply careful spending. If the "necessary" folder sails through unquestioned while the "wants" folder requires months of internal argument over a purchase your verified plan can easily absorb, the split isn't about the money. It's about which category earned the right to be spent on without a fight.

What it costs you

The direct cost is straightforward to name and easy to underestimate: entire categories of quality of life — hobbies, comfort, travel, the specific pleasures a person spent decades imagining they'd finally have time and money for — get systematically underfunded relative to a plan that could easily support them, not because the plan says no, but because an internal moral ledger, built long before retirement and never updated, keeps sorting personal enjoyment into a folder that has to justify itself every single time, while every other category sails through by default.

There's a subtler cost worth naming specifically for what it does to a retiree's relationship with their own judgment: the travel agent, a genuine expert on the value of experiential spending in later life, has effectively stopped trusting her own professional wisdom the moment it applies to her own account — a specific and quietly painful irony, watching herself decline exactly the advice she gave clients for a quarter century, unable to extend to herself the same permission she extended freely, for decades, to strangers. That gap between professional insight and personal application doesn't stay contained to spending; it tends to generalize into a broader, low-grade sense that she doesn't quite deserve the ease she spent her whole career helping other people access.

There's a compounding cost worth sitting with for anyone carrying this pattern into the later years of retirement specifically: many of the purchases sorted into the "frivolous" folder — travel while still healthy and mobile, a hobby requiring physical dexterity, an experience that depends on stamina — carry an expiration date that has nothing to do with the money and everything to do with the body. A furnace can be replaced at any age. A trip requiring a full day of walking, or a hobby requiring steady hands, cannot always be deferred indefinitely without quietly losing the physical capacity to enjoy it at all. Four months of deliberation over the woodworking tools costs the machinist four months of his hands' current dexterity, four months he does not get back regardless of how the deliberation eventually resolves.

The court reporter's cost is worth saying outright for a different reason: a two-year-old subscription to a lecture series, never purchased, isn't a large sum of money by any measure, and it would be easy to dismiss it as too minor to matter. But her list contains not one deferred purchase but an entire category of them, accumulated silently across years of the same rule running unexamined — a pattern that, added up, represents a meaningfully sized slice of a life spent declining things a decades-old rule never actually had the authority to keep declining on her behalf.

There's a final cost worth flagging across all three of this chapter's scenes, because it concerns something the dollar figures alone don't capture: the specific, quiet loneliness of maintaining a private moral ledger nobody else in the household ever agreed to. The machinist's wife would have told him, instantly, that the woodworking tools were an easy yes. The travel agent's daughter would have told her mother the same about the trip. The court reporter's own list was never actually reviewed or endorsed by anyone else in her life — it was built alone, decades ago, and has been enforced alone, in silence, ever since. A rule nobody else was ever asked to weigh in on carries a particular kind of authority precisely because it's never been tested against another person's honest reaction, and every chapter in this book that involves this specific dynamic is, in part, an argument for finally testing it.

The overrides

Rename the folders, deliberately, to reflect what your verified plan actually says. "Necessary" and "frivolous" are not financial categories — they're inherited moral labels wearing financial language. Replace them, explicitly and in writing, with the only two categories your plan actually recognizes: "within the verified budget" and "outside the verified budget." A furnace and a set of woodworking tools, both comfortably inside the verified budget, belong in the identical category under this relabeling, whatever their old moral folder used to say.

Assign legitimacy to the personal purchase the same way an obligation receives it. The furnace gets its legitimacy from an external event — it broke, a bill arrived, the decision was made for you. Personal spending rarely arrives with that kind of external permission slip attached, which is precisely why it's so much easier to defer indefinitely. Create your own version of the external trigger: a standing, calendar-based "personal spending day" each quarter, treated with the same non-negotiable weight as a bill's due date, where a specific, pre-approved category of personal spending simply happens, the way the furnace payment simply happens, without requiring fresh permission each time.

The Move: apply your own best professional or life judgment to your own account, explicitly, as if evaluating a friend's situation instead of your own. The travel agent already knows, with real expertise, that travel while healthy is a valuable use of retirement money — she has just never granted her own account the benefit of that expertise. Write down, specifically, what you would tell a close friend in your exact financial position who was hesitating over the same purchase you're currently deferring. Most people carrying this reflex find they already know the correct answer; they've simply never been willing to give it to themselves directly.

Track spending by category over a full year, not by individual purchase. A single, isolated deliberation over one purchase makes the moral weighting feel proportionate and reasonable in the moment. A full year's tally, showing exactly how much went into the effortless "obligations" folder versus the contested "wants" folder, relative to what the verified plan allocates to each, tends to make the imbalance obvious in a way no single purchase ever fully reveals on its own.

Formally retire the old list, the same way a rule you wrote yourself deserves a formal repeal. For a pattern like the court reporter's, where the category was consciously built rather than passively absorbed, the fix benefits from equal formality on the other end. Write out the original list, name the circumstances it was built for, and cross it out, deliberately, once those circumstances have genuinely changed — the same ceremony a person would give any other rule that had clearly done its job and earned retirement of its own.

Eight months after the shoulder massage decision described in the previous chapter, the machinist finally buys the woodworking tools — not because the four-month internal argument resolved on its own, but because his daughter, having heard the story, asks him directly what he'd tell her if their positions were reversed. He tells her, without hesitation, that she should absolutely buy them. He hears himself say it. He orders the tools that same week, and reports back to her, a month later, that he's been in the garage most evenings since, and that the whole four months of deliberation now strikes him as faintly ridiculous, the way an old, resolved argument often does in hindsight.

The court reporter, a few weeks after formally crossing out her old list, finally subscribes to the lecture series — a small purchase, in dollar terms, that she describes to a friend as feeling oddly ceremonial, like closing a file she'd left open for two years without quite noticing. She adds, half-joking, that the list had been so specific and so confidently held that she'd forgotten it was ever a decision at all rather than simply a fact about who she was. Crossing it out, on paper, turned out to matter more than she expected it to.

The Rule to Remember: your account doesn't sort spending into "necessary" and "frivolous." You do — and the sorting was never really about the price tag. It was about which purchases you'd already decided you were allowed to want.

Chapter 5 — The Job You Can't Stop Doing

A retired university administrator, a woman who spent nineteen years as a dean overseeing a large academic division, agrees, four months into retirement, to take on a "small" consulting project for her former institution — a part-time review of a departmental restructuring, a handful of hours a week, unpaid, framed by everyone involved, including her, as simply staying connected to a community she cares about. Eight months later, the handful of hours has become something closer to a part-time job, unpaid, unstructured, quietly filling the exact hours she'd spent the last several years of her career telling herself she couldn't wait to finally have back. Her husband, gently, asks her one evening why she took on a second, unpaid version of the job she'd just spent nineteen years being genuinely ready to leave. She doesn't have a clean answer. What she has, instead, is a specific and hard-to-name discomfort that arrives on the mornings she doesn't have anything scheduled — a formlessness to the day that the consulting work, whatever else it costs her, reliably fills.

A retired construction foreman, six years into what was supposed to be a full retirement, has taken three separate part-time jobs since leaving his primary career — a few months managing a small crew for a neighbor's home addition, a stretch consulting informally on a friend's commercial project, most recently a couple of shifts a week at a hardware store's contractor desk, a job that pays a fraction of what he made running crews for three decades. None of these jobs are financially necessary; his pension and savings, verified by an advisor twice, comfortably support a retirement with no additional income at all. When his son asks why he keeps taking work that pays so little relative to what he used to earn, he says he "just likes staying busy" — true, as far as it goes, but incomplete in a way that becomes clearer once you notice what, specifically, he seems unable to tolerate about the alternative: a week with no defined role in it at all, no clear answer, if a stranger asked, to the question of what he does.

A retired orchestra conductor offers a third, quieter version of the same pattern, distinct in shape from the other two. He hasn't taken on paid or unpaid work since retiring, and by every outward measure his transition looks clean and complete. But he has continued, three years in, to attend every rehearsal of the ensemble he used to lead, sitting in the back rows, unasked, offering notes to the new conductor whenever the opportunity arises. The new conductor is polite about it, and privately, increasingly, uncomfortable. The old conductor doesn't experience himself as unable to let go — he'd describe his presence as simply loving the music, wanting to stay involved. What he can't quite see is that his physical presence in that specific room, week after week, is less about the music than about a role he has not yet found anywhere else to occupy, and that the ensemble he built has become, without either party quite naming it, the last place he still gets to be the person he spent four decades becoming.

What's actually happening

All three of these people are demonstrating a version of this book's core mechanism that doesn't touch spending directly at all — it operates one layer upstream, on the identity that made earning, and by extension controlled spending, feel meaningful in the first place. The reflex this book describes isn't only about money. For a very large number of people, it's inseparable from a working identity that took decades to build, and retirement doesn't just remove an income source. It removes the role that income source was attached to, and the role, it turns out, is often what people are actually struggling to let go of — the money is simply the most visible symptom.

There's a well-established framework in gerontology, developed by the sociologist Robert Atchley across research published from the late 1980s onward, called continuity theory. Atchley's research, based on extensive study of how people actually adapt to the retirement transition, found that psychological well-being in retirement correlates strongly with a person's ability to maintain continuity with their pre-retirement identity, activities, and sense of purpose — not by refusing to retire in any practical sense, but by finding ways to carry forward the internal structure, the sense of contribution and competence, that the working role used to provide externally. Atchley's framework helps explain why the dean and the foreman both, independently, reached for informal, low-paid or unpaid versions of their old professional roles rather than simply enjoying unstructured time: retirement without some deliberate continuity plan doesn't just remove a paycheck. It removes an entire external scaffolding of purpose, competence, and daily structure that both of them had spent decades building their sense of self around, and the discomfort of that scaffolding's absence, not any actual financial need, is what's driving the reflex to quietly rebuild a version of it.

A closely related concept, developed by the psychologists Hazel Markus and Paula Nurius in their influential 1986 paper, is useful here: the idea of "possible selves" — the specific, vivid mental images people carry of who they might become, including both hoped-for versions of the self and feared ones. For someone who spent decades as a dean, a foreman, or in any role that became genuinely central to their identity, "retired person with no defined role" often exists, if it exists at all in their imagination, as one of the feared possible selves rather than a hoped-for one — an identity that reads, internally, as closer to obsolescence than to freedom, regardless of how the retirement was actually planned or how comfortably it's funded. The consulting project and the hardware store shifts function, in this light, as active avoidance of stepping into that feared possible self, even at the cost of the actual, hoped-for retirement both of them spent years imagining and planning for.

It's worth being precise about how this identity-level reflex connects back to the book's central mechanism around spending specifically, because the connection is real even though it isn't obvious at first. A person who cannot fully let go of an income-producing role, even an unpaid or low-paid one, is often, underneath the surface explanation of "staying busy," managing the exact same discomfort this book's earlier chapters describe — the discomfort of a life with no active income source, addressed here not by restricting withdrawals from savings, but by trying to prevent the paycheck-shaped structure from fully disappearing in the first place. The dean's consulting work and the foreman's contractor-desk shifts are, in this sense, a different channel for the identical underlying reflex covered elsewhere in this book: rather than tightening a budget or refusing a withdrawal, the reflex here works to keep the old rule — money still arriving from effort — technically true, even in symbolic or heavily discounted form, because the alternative, full decumulation with no income of any kind coming in, is the actual thing being avoided.

The conductor's version doesn't even carry a symbolic income component, which makes it useful for seeing the identity mechanism in its purest form, isolated from any question of money at all. He has no compensation attached to his continued presence in that rehearsal room, no financial reason of any kind to keep showing up. What he's defending isn't a paycheck-shaped structure — it's the role itself, stripped down to its bare form: being the person whose opinion about the music in that room carries weight. Atchley's continuity theory would predict exactly this kind of behavior from someone whose professional identity was this central to their sense of self for this many decades, and it would also predict, correctly, that the behavior tends to persist until a genuine, deliberately chosen alternative source of that same kind of contribution is found — not because the person is unusually stubborn, but because the underlying need for competence and contribution doesn't go anywhere just because the job that used to supply it ended.

It's worth stating plainly, too, a specific structural reason retirement is a harder identity transition than most of the career changes a person navigates during their working years. A job change, even an involuntary one, typically preserves the broader category "employed person" — the identity shifts in its particulars but not in its fundamental shape. Retirement removes the category itself, not just the particulars within it, which is a considerably larger identity disruption than most working-life transitions ever require. Atchley's research specifically distinguishes retirement from ordinary job change on exactly this basis, which is part of why continuity theory treats it as its own distinct area of study rather than simply one more instance of career transition research. The dean and the foreman aren't struggling with an unusually large dose of an ordinary problem. They're navigating a structurally different kind of change than almost anything else either of them faced across their entire working lives.

How to tell the difference. Plenty of retirees genuinely enjoy part-time work, consulting, or informal projects for reasons that have nothing to do with this reflex — real enjoyment of the work itself, a desire for social connection, or simply liking to stay engaged with a field they spent decades mastering. The distinguishing question isn't whether the work is present, but whether stopping it feels available as a real option. If a retiree could walk away from the part-time role at any point without a specific, identifiable discomfort driving them to replace it with something similar, the work is likely a genuine preference. If the role keeps reappearing, in slightly different forms, each time an unstructured stretch opens up, and if the person struggles to articulate any concrete reason for continuing it beyond a vague need to "stay busy," that vagueness itself is often the clue — a specific, well-reasoned preference for engaging work usually comes with specific, well-reasoned language. A reflex managing an identity vacuum usually doesn't.

What it costs you

The most direct cost is the one hiding in plain sight in both scenes above: the actual retirement, the one that was planned for and saved toward and looked forward to across decades, keeps getting quietly deferred in favor of a diminished, unpaid or underpaid echo of the career that was supposed to be finished. The dean isn't living the retirement her verified plan supports. She's living a part-time, unpaid extension of her old job, with none of its former compensation or authority, and very little of the actual rest either of the two roles was supposed to eventually provide.

There's a cost specific to what this pattern does to a marriage or a partnership, worth calling out directly: the foreman's wife, and the dean's husband, both planned, across years of anticipation, for a retirement that included their spouse's actual presence and attention — not a spouse who is technically home but functionally still managing a version of their old job, still mentally at the job site or the department even while physically at the kitchen table. The cost isn't only the retiree's own unlived life. It's the partner's unlived shared retirement, quietly diminished by a role neither of them ever explicitly agreed the retiree would keep.

There's a longer-term cost worth pointing out as well: continuity theory suggests that retirees who never develop a genuine, deliberate alternative source of purpose and structure

— who instead simply keep patching the old role back together in smaller and smaller pieces for as long as their health allows — tend to experience a much harder transition whenever health, mobility, or opportunity eventually forces the patched-together role to end entirely. The dean and the foreman are, in effect, postponing the actual work of building a new identity, and postponing it does not make that work smaller. It usually makes it larger, and it guarantees the eventual reckoning happens later in life, with fewer years and less energy available to do it well.

The conductor's cost is relational in a way worth noting directly directly, because it extends beyond his own unlived retirement into an institution and a relationship he genuinely cares about. The new conductor's discomfort, unaddressed, is quietly eroding what could otherwise be a valuable mentoring relationship between the two of them, and the ensemble itself is not getting the clean, full transition of leadership it needs to fully become the new conductor's own. None of this is what the old conductor intends. But intention isn't the variable doing the damage here — presence is, and presence, however lovingly meant, is not currently his to keep offering on the old terms.

The overrides

Name the feared possible self directly, in specific language. Markus and Nurius's research suggests that vague, unexamined fears about a future identity carry more power than fears that have been named precisely. Instead of a general unease about "not having a role," write down the specific, concrete image underneath it — what, exactly, does "retired with no defined role" look like in your imagination, and what specifically about that image feels threatening. Naming it precisely is often the first step toward discovering the feared image is considerably less accurate, and less inevitable, than it felt while it stayed vague.

Build a deliberate continuity plan before drifting into an accidental one. Atchley's continuity theory doesn't argue against staying engaged after retirement — it argues for choosing the form that engagement takes on purpose, rather than defaulting into the nearest available echo of the old career simply because it's familiar. A volunteer role, a genuinely new skill, a creative project, or even paid consulting work chosen deliberately for reasons you can articulate clearly — all of these can provide the same continuity benefit Atchley's research documents, without requiring the retiree to remain, functionally, still employed in the exact shape of the job they meant to leave.

The Move: schedule the unstructured time before it has a chance to feel like a vacuum. Both the dean and the foreman describe the discomfort arriving specifically on days with nothing scheduled — the formlessness itself, not any particular financial worry, is what the old role's echo is filling. Building deliberate structure into unstructured time — a standing weekly commitment to something genuinely new, chosen for its own value rather than as an escape from open time — removes the vacuum the old identity keeps rushing back in to fill.

Distinguish the loss you're grieving from the identity you're defending, and give each its own real space. Some part of what all three of this chapter's figures are managing is genuine, legitimate grief for a role that mattered and is now, correctly, over — and grief deserves acknowledgment, not just a behavioral workaround. Separating the two — a real, worth-honoring loss on one hand, and an active, still-changeable identity reflex on the other — keeps the overrides in this chapter from accidentally asking a reader to skip past something that actually deserves to be felt, on the way to something that also, separately, needs to be changed.

Ask what the old role actually provided, piece by piece, and replace each piece deliberately. A career rarely provides just one thing. It usually provides several — structure, competence, social contact, a sense of contribution, external validation — bundled together in a single package. Unbundling them, and asking which specific pieces are actually missing, makes it possible to replace each one with something built for the purpose, rather than reaching for the whole old bundle at once simply because it's the only bundle you know how to build.

Find the smallest available version of the missing piece before assuming you need the whole role back. Often what's actually missing isn't the job itself but one specific ingredient inside it — being asked a genuine question by someone younger, for instance, or simply being in a room where competence is visible and valued. The conductor's eventual chamber group met that need in miniature, without requiring anything like his former authority over an entire institution. Identifying the smallest sufficient version of what's missing, before reaching for a full-scale replacement of the old role, often produces a better fit with considerably less collateral cost to the people still occupying the position you left.

Create a formal ending, even where none was required. The dean's and the foreman's transitions each had a clear last day; the conductor's didn't, because nothing about his relationship to the ensemble was ever formally structured to end, which is part of why it has simply continued by default. A deliberate closing ritual — a final address to the ensemble, an honest conversation with the new conductor about stepping back, a specific date after which his attendance changes to something clearly bounded, like one concert a season as an honored guest rather than a weekly presence — gives an unbounded, ambiguous role the same clean edge a formal retirement date gave to his career.

The dean, six months after her husband's question at the kitchen table, ends the consulting arrangement — not abruptly, but with a clear conversation and a real transition plan for the department. In its place, she commits to two mornings a week tutoring undergraduates at a community college near her home, a role she chose specifically because it uses a piece of what she misses — mentorship, competence, contact with students — without functioning as an unpaid extension of the exact job she'd already, correctly, decided to leave. She tells her husband, a few months in, that the mornings feel different in a way she has trouble naming precisely — lighter, she eventually settles on, though she isn't sure that's quite the right word either.

The conductor, after a long, honest conversation with the new conductor he'd been quietly overshadowing, agrees to a formal arrangement: one concert a season as a guest of honor, invited rather than simply present, with no standing seat in the back rows the rest of the year. He tells a former colleague, months later, that the change felt like a genuine loss for the first few weeks — sharper, if anything, than the original retirement had. What surprised him was how quickly a new shape filled the space afterward: a small chamber group he'd never had time for during his working decades, made up of retired musicians roughly his own age, meeting weekly in a room with no institutional history attached to it at all.

The Rule to Remember: retirement doesn't remove your need for purpose. It removes the job that used to supply it for free — and if you don't choose what replaces it, some quieter version of the old job will choose for you.

Chapter 6 — The Advice You Hired and Won't Take

A retired dentist, three years into retirement, sits across from his financial advisor for what has become, by this point, an almost ritual conversation. The advisor pulls up the same projection she's shown him at each of their last four annual meetings — a projection that says, clearly, on a chart he understands perfectly well given his own decades of running a practice's finances, that he could increase his monthly spending by a meaningful margin and still, with extremely high confidence, never run out of money across his full projected lifespan, even accounting for a serious health event, even accounting for a bad decade in the markets. He nods along. He asks a few clarifying questions about the assumptions behind the projection, questions that are genuinely thoughtful and that the advisor answers to his evident satisfaction. He thanks her for the review. He leaves the meeting, as he has left the last four, and changes nothing about his actual monthly spending in the weeks and months that follow.

A retired librarian describes an almost identical dynamic to a friend, with a specific detail that makes the gap even more visible: her advisor, at their most recent meeting, actually printed out, in large font, a single sentence for her to take home — "you are financially able to spend approximately forty percent more each month than you currently do" — and suggested she tape it somewhere she'd see it regularly. She did tape it up, on the inside of a kitchen cabinet door, where she genuinely sees it several times a week. Eight months later, her spending hasn't moved. She reads the sentence, most times she sees it, with something like recognition — yes, that's what the numbers say — and then closes the cabinet and goes about her day exactly as she has for months, the sentence functioning less as an instruction she's following and more as a fact she's simply gotten used to living beside, unacted upon.

A retired pharmacist offers a third version of the same gap, notable because she works in a field defined by precise, evidence-based compliance and would, professionally, find a patient's failure to follow verified guidance genuinely puzzling. Her own advisor has recommended, for two consecutive years, a specific increase to her monthly spending that would let her finally address a kitchen she's disliked for a decade. She has, both years, said yes in the meeting, and both years, the increase never actually reached her monthly transfers. When her son, a physician, points out the irony — that she spent thirty years counseling patients on exactly this kind of gap between knowing a regimen and following it — she laughs, genuinely startled, and admits she'd never once applied her own professional framework for medication non-adherence to her own financial behavior, despite the parallel being, once named, almost uncomfortably exact.

What's actually happening

All three of these scenes describe a genuinely strange and specific gap — not a lack of information, and not distrust of the professional delivering it, but a persistent failure of information to convert into behavior, even when the information is clear, repeated, trusted, and in the librarian's case, literally taped to a cabinet door where it's seen every day. This gap is worth taking seriously on its own terms, because it points to something important about how this book's central reflex actually operates:

it does not live in the part of the mind that processes facts. It lives somewhere else entirely, and facts, however well presented, don't have direct access to that other location.

The economist George Loewenstein, working across several decades of research into what he termed the role of visceral factors in decision-making, has documented extensively how immediate, felt states — fear, craving, discomfort — can override even fully accurate information a person consciously accepts as true. Loewenstein's research draws a sharp distinction between "cold" cognitive knowledge — the kind that lives in a spreadsheet, a projection, a printed sentence on a cabinet door — and "hot" visceral states, which are activated in the moment of decision and often overpower cold cognition even when the person experiencing the override would readily agree, if asked directly and calmly, that the cold information is correct. The dentist isn't disputing his advisor's math. He accepts it completely, in the cold, calm setting of an annual review. What overrides the math isn't a competing fact. It's a felt, visceral discomfort that activates specifically in the moment of actually authorizing a larger withdrawal — a moment the calm, seated conversation with the advisor never quite replicates, which is precisely why the advice can be accepted intellectually at the meeting and still fail to translate into behavior once the meeting ends and the actual withdrawal decision has to be made alone.

This connects directly to a well-documented pattern in behavioral economics called present bias, or hyperbolic discounting — research developed substantially by the economist David Laibson across the 1990s and 2000s, building on earlier observations, which describes the finding that people consistently value immediate outcomes disproportionately relative to future ones, in a way that standard economic models of rational, consistent discounting fail to predict. Present bias is usually discussed in the context of saving too little — the classic finding that people would rather have a smaller amount of money today than a meaningfully larger amount a year from now, even when a purely rational calculation favors waiting. But the same underlying bias operates, somewhat counterintuitively, in exactly the opposite direction for the reflex this book describes: the immediate, felt discomfort of authorizing a withdrawal right now is weighted more heavily than the abstract, future benefit of a fuller life enabled by that spending — a benefit that, however real and however well documented by the advisor's projection, lives in the future, and present bias, by its nature, discounts the future relative to the immediate present almost regardless of how well-supported that future benefit actually is.

There's a further wrinkle worth naming, because it explains something particular about why a printed sentence on a cabinet door, however clear, so rarely closes this specific gap on its own: cold cognitive information, in Loewenstein's framework, is genuinely useful for planning and for overriding visceral states that haven't yet activated — reading the sentence calmly, in a kitchen, with no active withdrawal decision pending, produces the mild, easy agreement the librarian describes. But that same cold information tends to lose much of its force at the precise moment it would actually need to act — the moment of authorizing a specific transfer, booking a specific trip, approving a specific purchase — because that moment activates the visceral state directly, and visceral states, once active, are considerably harder to argue with using information absorbed calmly at a different time, in a different state, days or weeks removed from the actual decision point.

The pharmacist's own professional field has a well-documented name for a strikingly parallel pattern, worth introducing here because she already, unknowingly, has expert-level intuition for it: medication non-adherence, a subject of extensive research in health psychology and pharmacy practice, describes the well-documented gap between a patient's clear, expressed intention to follow a prescribed regimen and their actual, observed behavior — a gap that research in the field has found is only weakly related to how well the patient understands or agrees with the reasoning behind the regimen. Patients who fully accept that a medication is necessary still, routinely, fail to take it as directed, for reasons closely related to what Loewenstein's visceral-factors research describes: the moment of taking a pill, or in this case authorizing a transfer, is governed by an in-the-moment state that a calm, prior agreement doesn't automatically carry into. The interventions that actually improve medication adherence in the research literature are rarely more information — patients already have that. They're structural: pill organizers, automated reminders tied to an existing daily cue, blister packs that make the correct behavior the path of least resistance. The parallel to this chapter's overrides, several of which follow exactly that structural logic, is not a coincidence.

It's worth noting, too, why the visceral-cognitive gap this chapter describes tends to widen rather than narrow the longer a retiree has been retired, which runs counter to what most people would predict. Intuition suggests that more time living inside a verified plan, watching it perform exactly as projected, should gradually ease the discomfort of acting on it. What Loewenstein's broader research on habituation and visceral response suggests instead is that the visceral state activated at the moment of withdrawal doesn't reliably fade just because the cold information behind it has been repeatedly confirmed; without a deliberate intervention, the same discomfort can simply keep firing, fresh, at every single decision point, for years, regardless of how much accumulated evidence sits on the cognitive side of the ledger. The dentist's fourth consecutive year of nodding along and changing nothing isn't an anomaly. It's close to the expected outcome for a gap this chapter describes, absent one of the concrete overrides below.

How to tell the difference. A retiree who hasn't increased their spending because they genuinely disagree with an advisor's projection — perhaps they're carrying a risk the advisor hasn't fully weighted, or planning for an expense the projection doesn't account for — is exercising legitimate judgment, not this chapter's reflex. The distinguishing signature here is agreement without follow-through: the retiree who, when asked directly, confirms they trust the numbers, understands the reasoning, and have no specific counter-argument, and who still, months or years later, hasn't acted on what they've repeatedly agreed is true. If you can articulate a real, specific reason for disagreeing with your plan, that's a conversation to have with your advisor, not a pattern to override. If your only honest answer is some version of "I know, I just can't quite bring myself to," that's the visceral-cognitive gap this chapter describes.

What it costs you

The most immediate cost is the literal one: years of professionally verified, safely available spending capacity going unused, not because the advice was wrong or poorly delivered, but because knowing and doing turned out to require two entirely different kinds of work, and only one of them was ever actually addressed by the advisory relationship. Three years of the dentist's retirement, and eight months of the librarian's, have already passed with a meaningful, verified gap between what could have funded a fuller life and what actually did, and neither of them is any closer to closing that gap through additional information alone, because additional information was never the missing ingredient.

There's a specific and somewhat painful cost worth sitting with for what this gap does to the value of the advisory relationship itself: both of these retirees are, in effect, paying for professional guidance they aren't using, which is not merely inefficient but genuinely demoralizing over time for both the retiree and, often, for the advisor delivering the same unheeded projection year after year. An advisory relationship that produces accurate information without producing corresponding behavior eventually starts to feel, to the retiree, like an annual reminder of a gap they can't seem to close, rather than the useful, empowering resource it was meant to be — which risks the retiree eventually disengaging from the relationship altogether, precisely the outcome least likely to help.

There's a broader cost worth saying outright as well: the visceral-cognitive gap this chapter describes doesn't only cost money left unspent. It costs a retiree's confidence in their own capacity for follow-through, in a domain — their own financial life — where that confidence used to be hard-earned and genuinely justified. A person who spent decades successfully executing complex financial decisions in a demanding career can find themselves, in retirement, unable to execute a single, simple, professionally verified spending decision, and the resulting sense of "something is wrong with me specifically" is itself a real cost, compounding the financial one with an emotional one that has nothing to do with actual capability and everything to do with a mismatch this chapter has been naming throughout.

For the pharmacist specifically, there's an added cost worth flagging: two consecutive years of the identical unfollowed recommendation is not a minor lapse for someone whose entire career was organized around helping other people close exactly this gap. The kitchen she's disliked for a decade remains disliked, but the sharper cost is quieter — a professional who spent thirty years never judging a patient for a struggle she now recognizes, uncomfortably, as her own, and who has to sit with the specific humility of that recognition before she can actually apply her own well-earned expertise to herself.

There's a shared, cumulative cost worth stating plainly across all three of this chapter's scenes: an advisory relationship that produces accurate, repeated, unheeded advice year after year eventually risks becoming a source of quiet guilt in its own right, entirely apart from the money involved. The dentist, the librarian, and the pharmacist each describe some version of mild dread heading into their annual reviews — not because the news is ever bad, but because each meeting has become, without anyone intending it, a fresh occasion to confront a gap none of them has yet closed. A relationship meant to provide reassurance and clarity has, for all three, taken on a faint undertone of report-card anxiety, which is a strange and avoidable cost for a service they are, in every case, paying good money to receive.

The overrides

Bring the withdrawal into the room with the advisor, not just the projection. Instead of ending each meeting with an agreement about what could be spent, end it with an actual, specific transaction authorized in the room, in the advisor's presence, before the visceral discomfort has a chance to reassert itself once the meeting ends. Loewenstein's research on visceral states suggests the gap between knowing and doing widens with time and distance from the decision point; closing that gap means acting inside the low-friction moment the meeting itself provides, rather than deferring the action to a later moment when the discomfort will have full authority again.

Pair the cold information with a warm trigger. A printed sentence on a cabinet door delivers cold, accurate information at a moment with no active decision attached to it — which is exactly why it fails to translate. Pair the information instead with the actual moment of decision: a sticky note on the specific account login screen, not the cabinet door, so the fact arrives at the precise moment the visceral state activates, rather than at a calm moment hours or days removed from it.

The Move: pre-authorize a specific, recurring increase, once, rather than re-deciding every month. Present bias weighs each individual decision moment heavily in favor of the immediate, comfortable status quo — which means a retiree re-litigating the spending decision every single month will lose to the reflex almost every time, even while genuinely agreeing with the advisor's numbers each time they're presented. A single, one-time decision — made once, in the advisor's presence, to set a new, higher recurring transfer — removes the need to win the same visceral argument over and over, converting an infinite series of monthly battles into a single decision that, once made, doesn't require repeated willpower to sustain.

Track the gap explicitly, and review it as its own line item. Most advisory relationships track whether a plan remains on target financially. Few explicitly track the size of the gap between verified capacity and actual behavior. Asking your advisor to track and report that specific gap, meeting after meeting, turns an invisible, easily rationalized pattern into a visible, cumulative number — one that tends to become harder to keep ignoring once it's been named and quantified across several consecutive reviews rather than treated as a fresh, forgettable conversation each time.

Separate the meeting where you agree from the moment where you act, and shrink the gap between them to zero when possible. Much of this chapter's gap survives because agreement and action are allowed to happen in two different settings, days or weeks apart, with the visceral state getting a full run at the decision in between. Wherever practical, collapse that gap: authorize the change in the same sitting where you agreed to it, before leaving the room, before the calm cognitive agreement has a chance to be outlasted by the visceral resistance waiting for you at home.

Borrow the adherence toolkit directly, structural piece by structural piece. If medication non-adherence research has already solved a closely parallel version of this exact problem, use its solutions rather than reinventing them. A recurring calendar reminder tied to an existing daily habit, a visible physical cue at the moment of decision, a specific accountability check-in with another person — the pharmacist's own professional field has spent decades refining exactly these tools for exactly this kind of intention-behavior gap, and there's no reason the toolkit stops working simply because the "regimen" in question is a monthly transfer instead of a prescription.

The librarian's advisor, at their next meeting, suggests exactly this: rather than another printed sentence, they set up, together, in the room, a modest, automatic increase to her recurring monthly transfer — nothing dramatic, well short of the full forty percent, but a real, specific, executed change rather than another piece of information to carry home and tape to a cabinet. Three months later, at a follow-up check-in, her spending has, for the first time in years, actually moved to match a number her advisor recommended. She tells her friend it felt strange for about two weeks and then simply became the new normal, in the specific and slightly anticlimactic way most successfully adopted changes eventually do.

The pharmacist, at her next annual review, asks her advisor to set up exactly the kind of structural intervention her own field would recommend for a patient in her position — an automated increase tied to a fixed date, agreed to in the room, requiring no further monthly decision. She tells her son, the physician, about it afterward with a kind of wry recognition, noting that she'd counseled hundreds of patients through exactly this kind of fix over three decades and never once thought to prescribe it to herself until the parallel was named out loud.

The Rule to Remember: knowing what your plan supports and doing what your plan supports are two different skills — and no amount of additional knowing will ever substitute for the one decision that actually does the doing.

Chapter 7 — The Disaster That Keeps Almost Happening

A retired Army officer, five years into retirement after a full career of genuinely high-stakes planning, has built, in the years since leaving service, an elaborate and constantly updated set of contingency scenarios for his retirement finances — a long-term-care event requiring a level of paid support well beyond what his and his wife's health currently suggests either of them will need, a market collapse considerably more severe than any downturn in the historical record his advisor's projections are built on, a sudden and total loss of one of their two pension sources despite both being backed by institutions with no history of default. None of these scenarios are impossible in the strictest sense — nothing is truly impossible — but each one is individually unlikely, and his verified plan already includes a reasonable, professionally calibrated margin for ordinary bad luck. He maintains all three scenarios anyway, revisiting and updating them regularly, and uses their combined, worst-case weight to justify keeping his actual monthly spending well below what his plan comfortably supports even under considerably less rosy assumptions than the ones his advisor uses.

A retired hospital administrator, three years retired after a long career managing crisis response for a large regional health system, describes a related pattern with a specific professional flavor to it. She spent decades being, correctly and usefully, the person in the room who asked "what if this goes wrong" before any major institutional decision — a habit that served her hospital extremely well across multiple genuine emergencies over the years. In retirement, the habit hasn't found a new target to attach itself to; it has simply redirected, at full strength, onto her own household finances, generating a running, ever-present list of what-ifs that she treats with the same institutional seriousness she once brought to hospital-wide contingency planning, despite her own personal finances carrying nowhere near the scale or genuine unpredictability of a regional health system's operations.

A retired claims investigator offers a third version, distinct for how narrowly focused his particular worst case is compared to the officer's sprawling set of scenarios. He spent twenty-six years professionally trained to detect fraud, deception, and hidden risk in insurance claims — a career built entirely around assuming the story in front of him might not be the whole story. He has fixated, since retiring, on a single, specific fear: that his financial institution itself, despite decades of stability and federal deposit protections he can recite from memory, will somehow fail or be compromised, and he has responded by keeping a meaningfully large sum of cash, physically, in his home, money that would otherwise be safely invested and growing according to his verified plan, money that is now instead earning nothing and, statistically, sitting in a form considerably more vulnerable to loss than the institutional accounts he distrusts.

What's actually happening

All three of these patterns draw on a real and well-documented feature of human cognition, worth stating plainly honestly and precisely because it isn't a flaw exactly — it's a genuine adaptation that becomes miscalibrated when applied outside the context it evolved to handle. Psychologists have long documented what's often called negativity bias — a well-replicated finding, summarized comprehensively in a widely cited 2001 review paper by the psychologist Roy Baumeister and colleagues titled “Bad Is Stronger Than Good,” which found, across a wide range of domains, that negative events, emotions, and information consistently carry more psychological weight than positive ones of equivalent magnitude. This isn’t a personality quirk specific to the officer or the administrator. It’s a broadly shared feature of human cognition, present to some degree in nearly everyone, that historically served an obvious survival function: overweighting threats costs little when the threat is real and catastrophic when it’s missed, so a cognitive system biased toward taking negative possibilities seriously was, across most of human evolutionary history, a reasonably good bet.

What makes the officer’s and the administrator’s versions of this bias particularly stubborn is that both of them spent entire careers being professionally rewarded for exactly this kind of worst-case thinking — the officer’s planning genuinely did need to account for scenarios most people never have to consider, and the administrator’s crisis-response instincts genuinely did save lives at points across her career. Negativity bias, already a broadly shared human tendency, gets substantially reinforced and sharpened by decades of professional practice that specifically trains and rewards it, which means both of them are carrying not just an ordinary human tilt toward worst-case thinking, but a professionally honed, expert-level version of it — one that doesn't recognize, on its own, that the domain it's now being applied to has changed from an institution managing genuine, large-scale uncertainty to a personal retirement account with a verified, professionally calibrated safety margin already built in.

There's a related concept worth introducing that sharpens why the specific what-if scenarios keep multiplying rather than settling into a fixed, manageable list: research on what's sometimes called catastrophizing — a term used across cognitive-behavioral research to describe the tendency to generate and dwell on worst-case interpretations of ambiguous or uncertain situations — has found that catastrophizing tends to be self-reinforcing rather than self-limiting. Generating one worst-case scenario doesn't satisfy the underlying negativity bias; it tends to open the door to generating another, and then another, because each new scenario, however unlikely, feels like it's adding useful protective coverage rather than adding diminishing, and eventually counterproductive, returns. The officer's three scenarios aren't a complete, bounded list he's satisfied with. They're an ongoing project, continually updated and expanded, because the underlying bias driving their generation was never actually asking "what's the complete, realistic set of risks" — it was asking "what haven't I thought of yet," a question that, by its nature, never runs out of new candidate answers.

It's worth being direct about the real, legitimate function worst-case planning does serve, because this chapter isn't arguing that contingency planning itself is the problem — a verified retirement plan should, and typically does, already build in a reasonable margin for genuine bad luck, and nothing here should talk a reader out of maintaining real, sensible insurance and emergency reserves. The distinction this chapter is drawing is between planning that's bounded, specific, and already incorporated into the verified numbers versus planning that's unbounded, constantly regenerating, and used to justify spending well below what even a conservative, worst-case-adjusted version of the plan actually supports. The officer's advisor has already built long-term-care risk, market volatility, and pension-source diversification into the verified projection; the officer's ongoing, separate mental contingency planning is not adding real protection on top of that professional work. It's re-litigating, privately and without new information, a risk assessment a qualified professional has already completed.

The claims investigator's fixation is worth examining separately, because it illustrates something the officer's more diffuse pattern doesn't show as clearly: professional training doesn't just amplify negativity bias in general, it also shapes the specific content of the fear to match the exact domain the professional spent a career becoming expert in detecting. A career built around uncovering hidden risk in claims trained him, extremely well, to distrust surface-level reassurance and look for what isn't being said — an excellent instinct for fraud investigation, and a poorly calibrated one when aimed at a federally insured, heavily regulated financial institution operating under an entirely different risk profile than the fraudulent claims he spent decades uncovering. His fear isn't generic. It's a highly specific, professionally shaped worst case, mismatched to a domain that doesn't actually share the risk profile of the one his training was built to detect.

There's a further reason worth calling out for why professionals with genuine high-stakes experience are especially prone to this chapter's pattern, beyond the simple fact of trained vigilance. Baumeister's negativity-bias research also documents that negative experiences are encoded more vividly and are recalled more easily than positive ones of equal or even greater frequency — a genuine emergency the officer helped avert twenty years ago sits far more accessible in memory than the thousands of ordinary, uneventful days that surrounded it. A career spent occasionally, memorably encountering real catastrophe leaves behind a distorted internal sample of how often catastrophe actually occurs, weighted heavily toward the vivid exceptions rather than the far more numerous, forgettable ordinary days. Applied to retirement planning, this means the officer isn't drawing on an accurate internal database of how often financial disasters actually strike people in his position. He's drawing on a highly available, highly memorable, and highly unrepresentative sample of the worst days of an otherwise uneventful career.

How to tell the difference. A retiree who identifies a genuine, specific gap in their plan's risk coverage — an actual missing insurance product, an actual unaddressed health scenario the advisor hasn't priced in — is doing valuable, legitimate work, and should absolutely raise it with their advisor rather than dismissing the concern as this chapter's reflex. The distinguishing signature is whether the worst-case scenario has already been incorporated into the verified plan's margin. If your advisor has confirmed a specific risk is already accounted for in the plan's assumptions, and you continue to privately budget as though it isn't, that's this chapter's pattern. If a risk genuinely hasn't been discussed or priced into the plan at all, raising it is due diligence, not catastrophizing.

What it costs you

The most direct cost mirrors the pattern named throughout this book: real spending capacity, already verified and already accounting for a reasonable margin of bad luck, goes unused in service of protecting against risks that are, in most cases, already covered twice over — once by the plan's built-in margin, and again by the retiree's own separate, unofficial mental contingency budget stacked on top of it. The officer isn't protecting against one real risk. He's protecting against the same handful of risks multiple times over, in a way that provides no additional actual safety, only additional, unnecessary restriction.

There's a specific cost worth pointing out for what constant contingency planning does to the felt experience of retirement itself: a retirement spent perpetually rehearsing worst-case scenarios that never arrive is not a peaceful retirement, regardless of how sound the underlying account balance is. The administrator's household finances haven't experienced anything resembling the genuine emergencies her hospital career trained her to expect and manage — no market collapse beyond what her plan already anticipates, no health crisis beyond what her insurance already covers — and yet she reports, when asked honestly, that her retirement doesn't feel calm, because some part of her is still, most days, running crisis-response drills against threats that keep failing to materialize.

There's a relational cost worth noting directly as well, specific to both of these scenarios: constant, visible worst-case planning tends to transmit itself to a spouse or partner, whether or not that transmission is intended. The officer's wife has, over five years, absorbed a meaningful amount of his ongoing anxiety about scenarios that his own advisor has confirmed are already covered, not because she independently arrived at the same worry, but because sustained proximity to someone else's catastrophizing tends to raise a partner's own baseline anxiety, even when that partner would, on their own, have felt considerably more at ease.

The claims investigator's cost is unusually concrete and worth stating plainly: cash held physically outside a properly insured account earns nothing, loses purchasing power to inflation every year it sits, and carries genuine risks — theft, fire, simple loss — that his verified institutional accounts do not carry to anywhere near the same degree. His specific worst-case fear, in other words, hasn't just cost him unused growth. It has moved his money into a form that is measurably less safe than the one he was trying to protect himself from, a precise and almost ironic illustration of how negativity bias, left unchecked, can manufacture the exact outcome it was trying to prevent.

There's a final, shared cost worth naming across all three of this chapter's scenes: worst-case planning, left unbounded, doesn't just fail to add real protection. It actively consumes the exact resource — time, attention, calm — that a well-funded retirement is supposed to free up in the first place. The officer, the administrator, and the claims investigator each spent decades in careers that legitimately demanded this kind of vigilance, and each has earned, by any fair measure, a retirement where that particular muscle finally gets to rest. None of them have given it that rest. The muscle is still working, every day, against threats that keep failing to justify the ongoing exertion, at the exact stage of life when the ability to finally set it down was supposed to become available.

The overrides

Take the unofficial contingency list to the actual advisor, once, and close it formally. Most of what's driving the ongoing, self-generated worst-case planning is the absence of an authoritative, external confirmation that the scenario has already been considered. Bringing the specific list — the long-term-care scenario, the severe-market scenario, the pension-loss scenario — to an actual professional review, and getting an explicit, written confirmation of whether and how each one is already priced into the plan, converts an open-ended, self-perpetuating private project into a closed, externally verified one.

Set a hard limit on new scenario generation. Catastrophizing research suggests the pattern is self-reinforcing precisely because it has no natural stopping point. Impose an artificial one: a fixed number of contingency scenarios, reviewed and finalized once a year with the advisor, with a firm rule against adding new ones outside that annual review. This doesn't eliminate legitimate risk planning; it bounds it, converting an unlimited, ongoing source of anxiety into a scheduled, contained task with a clear beginning and end.

The Move: redirect the professional skill toward a bounded target with a genuine off switch. The officer's and the administrator's worst-case-planning instincts are real, valuable professional skills that simply lack an appropriate target in retirement. Rather than trying to suppress the instinct entirely, which is unlikely to succeed given how deeply it's trained, give it a legitimate, bounded outlet — volunteering with an organization that genuinely needs contingency and crisis planning, for instance — where the skill can be exercised at full strength on a target designed to absorb it, rather than continuing to run, unbounded, against a personal retirement account that was never built to need it.

Track how often the imagined disaster actually arrives. Keep a simple, ongoing record of every major worst-case scenario generated over a given period, and revisit it a year later to note how many of them actually occurred. Most people carrying this pattern have never done this exercise, because each new scenario feels urgent and specific in the moment it's generated and gets quietly replaced by the next one before its own track record can be observed. Seeing, in writing, that the vast majority of the scenarios from a year ago simply never happened is often more persuasive than any single conversation about probability.

Ask what evidence would actually change your mind, and check whether it already exists. A useful test for distinguishing legitimate risk assessment from unbounded catastrophizing: name, specifically, what verified information would resolve the concern completely, and then check whether that information is already available and simply hasn't been consulted. The officer's advisor's projection, the administrator's institution's actual claims history, the investigator's bank's actual deposit-insurance documentation — in each case, the resolving evidence already existed, sitting unexamined, while the private mental scenario kept running in its place.

Match the fear to its actual domain, explicitly, before accepting it as valid. The claims investigator's fear is professionally shaped, which means the antidote is professionally specific: sitting down with someone who can speak with real authority to the actual risk profile of a federally insured institution, in the same detailed, evidence-based register his own career trained him to respect, rather than a general reassurance he's likely to discount the way he'd discount an unsubstantiated claim. A fear built by expertise often only yields to a counter-argument delivered with matching expertise.

The administrator, a year into keeping this kind of record at her daughter's suggestion, counts eleven distinct worst-case scenarios she'd generated and taken seriously enough to adjust her spending around, over the previous twelve months. None of the eleven occurred. She doesn't describe the exercise as having eliminated her worst-case thinking entirely — she still generates new scenarios regularly, she tells her daughter, because that instinct is simply how her mind has worked for thirty years. What's changed is that she now has a full year of evidence, in her own handwriting, that the scenarios and the actual outcomes have almost nothing to do with each other, and that evidence has started, gradually, to earn more weight than the scenarios themselves.

The claims investigator, after a detailed conversation with a bank representative who walks him, methodically and with real documentation, through exactly how federal deposit insurance actually works, moves the majority of the cash back into his verified accounts over the following month. He tells his daughter it wasn't the reassurance itself that finally landed — he'd heard versions of it before, in the abstract. It was being handed the actual evidence, in the same rigorous, fact-by-fact register he used to demand from every claim that crossed his desk, that finally let the old investigator in him stand down.

The Rule to Remember: the disaster your plan has already priced in doesn't need a second, private budget defending against it — and the version of you still bracing for it isn't protecting your retirement. It's spending it on a threat that already lost.

Chapter 8 — The Gift You Keep Not Giving Yourself

A retired real estate agent, four years into retirement, sends her granddaughter a check for a semester of study abroad the same afternoon her daughter mentions the opportunity over the phone — no hesitation, no spreadsheet consulted, no waiting period, just a genuine, immediate pleasure in being able to say yes to something that will meaningfully change a young person's year. The following week, she cancels a long weekend trip to see an old friend she hasn't visited in three years, a trip costing a small fraction of the check she wrote without a second thought, because it "felt like a lot to spend right now" — a sentence she says out loud to herself, in her own kitchen, with no apparent awareness of how strange it sounds next to the check she wrote seven days earlier for a considerably larger amount.

A retired postal worker describes an almost identical asymmetry to his brother over coffee. He has, over the past two years, quietly paid off a grandson's credit card debt, covered a niece's car repair, and contributed generously to a nephew's wedding — each decision made easily, warmly, without the extended deliberation that characterizes almost every purchase he considers making for himself. The same two years have included exactly one purchase for his own enjoyment: a modest fishing rod, bought on sale, that took him three separate visits to the store before he actually brought it home. When his brother points out the gap — thousands given away with ease, a fishing rod requiring three visits — he laughs, a little uncomfortably, and says he "never really thought about it that way."

A retired auto mechanic offers a third version of this asymmetry, notable for how it plays out entirely within a single relationship rather than across several. He has, over the years since retiring, quietly fixed his adult son's car engine twice, at no charge, parts included, a gift that easily runs into four figures each time and that he offers without a second thought, describing it simply as "what a father does." The same man has not replaced his own decade-old recliner, worn through at the arm and genuinely uncomfortable to sit in for more than twenty minutes, despite his wife pointing out, more than once, that a new one would cost less than either engine repair. He tells her he'll "get around to it," a phrase that has now outlasted the recliner's original upholstery.

What's actually happening

This chapter's version of the pattern is, in some ways, the most counterintuitive shape this book describes, because on its surface it looks like the opposite of the reflex the rest of this book has been naming — generosity, not restriction, flowing easily in one direction while restriction holds firm in another. But the underlying mechanism is closely related to the endowment effect introduced in Chapter 4, and it's worth tracing precisely why giving to someone else and spending on oneself can feel, to the same person, holding the identical account, like two entirely different categories of risk.

Money given to a grandchild, a niece, or a nephew immediately and completely leaves the giver's own mental ledger — it's no longer 'my money that might run out"; it becomes, instantly, someone else's resource, someone else's story, entirely separate from the giver's own ongoing sense of financial vulnerability. This isn't a trivial reframing. It genuinely changes the psychological category the money belongs to, and money that's exited the giver's own ledger doesn't trigger the loss-aversion response this book has traced throughout, because loss aversion, as documented by Kahneman and Tversky's prospect theory, is specifically calibrated to changes in a person's own reference point — their own balance, their own account, their own felt sense of what they hold. A gift completed removes the money from that reference point entirely and instantly. A purchase for oneself does not; the money stays inside the giver's own account, inside their own ongoing story about their own financial security, right up until the moment it's spent, and every moment of deliberation before that spending is a moment the loss-aversion system has to weigh in on directly, in a way it never gets the chance to when the money is simply, cleanly given away.

There's a second mechanism at work as well, connected to the identity material covered in Chapter 5: for many people who built their sense of self substantially around being a provider, a caretaker, or a reliable source of support for family, giving isn't experienced primarily as spending at all. It's experienced as an act that confirms and reinforces a core identity — "I am the kind of person who takes care of my family" — which means giving carries its own positive psychological reward independent of, and often stronger than, whatever discomfort the loss-aversion system would otherwise register. Spending on oneself carries no equivalent identity reinforcement for most people raised with a strong provider ethic; there's no comparably deep-seated internal narrative that says "I am the kind of person who treats myself well," because that particular identity was rarely, if ever, actively built or reinforced across a working life mostly oriented toward providing for others. The postal worker's ease in paying off his grandson's debt isn't really about the dollar amount at all. It's about which identity the spending confirms, and only one of the two categories — giving, not receiving — has spent a lifetime being actively reinforced.

The mechanic's version isolates the pattern down to its cleanest possible form, because both purchases in his case involve almost identical objects — mechanical repair, a fair amount of money, a comfort item — differing only in whose comfort is at stake. Two engine repairs for his son cost more, combined, than several years' worth of replacement recliners would. The gap isn't about affordability, generosity, or even really about the son at all. It's about which purchase gets to skip the internal argument, and "what a father does" turns out to be a considerably more powerful, pre-approved script than anything available for "what a retired man gets to do for his own aching back."

It's worth sitting with the specific irony sitting inside this pattern, because it sharpens why it's worth taking seriously rather than simply admiring as generosity: a retiree who gives easily while restricting their own spending is not, typically, protecting their family's financial future more effectively than a retiree who spends more evenly across both categories. In most of the cases this book is describing, the verified plan comfortably supports both the giving and the personal spending — the real constraint isn't financial capacity at all, it's the asymmetric psychological weighting of the two categories, meaning the retiree isn't actually choosing family over self based on the numbers. They're choosing the category that doesn't trigger loss aversion over the category that does, and mistaking that psychological ease for a considered financial decision.

It's worth pausing on a related finding from moral psychology that sharpens why giving specifically, rather than any other category of spending, so reliably escapes the loss-aversion response this book has traced throughout. Researchers studying prosocial spending, including work by the psychologists Elizabeth Dunn and Michael Norton across the 2000s and 2010s, have found that spending money on others reliably produces greater reported happiness than spending an equivalent amount on oneself, across a wide range of cultures and income levels — a genuine, well-documented psychological benefit, not merely a moral obligation people grudgingly discharge. This helps explain why the asymmetry this chapter describes is so durable and so pleasant to maintain: giving isn't just exempt from loss aversion, it's actively, independently rewarding in its own right, which means the retiree isn't simply failing to notice the imbalance. They're being genuinely, doubly reinforced toward one side of it, while the other side offers no comparable reward to compete against the discomfort blocking it.

How to tell the difference. A retiree who gives generously and also spends comfortably on themselves, in roughly proportionate measure to what their plan supports, is not carrying this reflex — some people simply, genuinely enjoy giving more than they enjoy personal spending, and that's a legitimate preference, not a pattern requiring correction. The signature here is specifically the asymmetry: large, easy, undeliberated gifts to others sitting alongside small, heavily deliberated, frequently declined purchases for oneself, with the gap between the two categories' ease clearly disproportionate to their actual relative size or importance.

What it costs you

The most direct cost is one this book has already named in earlier chapters, applied here to a specific and often-overlooked category: an entire dimension of a retiree's own quality of life — comfort, connection with old friends, small pleasures, physical ease — goes systematically underfunded, not because the money isn't available, but because that particular category never developed the identity-level or psychological permission that giving to others receives automatically.

There's a subtler cost worth saying outright specifically for its effect on the giver's relationship with their own family: children and grandchildren who watch a parent or grandparent decline modest personal pleasures while giving generously to others often come away with real, quiet discomfort about the pattern, even when they're the ones receiving the generosity. The real estate agent's daughter, watching her mother cancel a modest visit to an old friend the same week she funded a semester abroad without hesitation, doesn't feel more grateful for the gift. She feels a specific, uncomfortable guilt about having asked for it at all, a guilt that has nothing to do with the actual math and everything to do with witnessing the visible imbalance up close.

There's a longer-term cost worth flagging as well, connected to earlier chapters' discussion of the years a retirement actually has available to be enjoyed: gifts given to grandchildren can typically be given at almost any point across a long retirement, with relatively little cost to delaying by a year or two if genuinely necessary. Personal pleasures that depend on the retiree's own current health, mobility, and available years — the trip to see the old friend, the physical activities requiring stamina, the experiences that specifically require the retiree's own continued vitality — do not carry the same flexibility. Consistently prioritizing the more delay-tolerant category over the less delay-tolerant one is, whether intended this way or not, a systematic bias against the exact category of spending most vulnerable to simply running out of time.

The mechanic's decade-old recliner carries a cost worth stating plainly directly, because it's the kind of cost that's easy to dismiss as trivial precisely because it's physical rather than financial: twenty minutes of discomfort, most evenings, for years, compounding into a genuinely significant quantity of unnecessary physical strain on a body that already spent decades doing hard, demanding manual work. A four-figure engine repair, given twice without hesitation, and a two-hundred-dollar chair, never bought, are not proportionate responses to two comparably real needs. They're proportionate to two very differently authorized categories, and only one of those two people in the household is currently living with the actual physical consequence of the imbalance every single evening.

There's a final cost worth calling out across all three of this chapter's scenes, tied to something the overrides below take seriously: every one of these three retirees is, in some real sense, already a generous, capable person who has simply never extended that same generosity across the specific line separating "others" from "self." That isn't a minor character detail. It means none of the fixes below require building a new capacity from nothing — the capacity for warm, unhesitating giving already exists, fully developed, in each of them. The actual work is narrower and more achievable than it might first appear: not becoming a more generous person, but becoming one who counts as eligible for the generosity that was already, demonstrably, there all along.

The overrides

Apply the giving standard to yourself, explicitly, as a test. Before declining a personal purchase, ask directly: would I hesitate this long if this exact amount were a request from my grandchild instead of a want of my own? If the honest answer is no — if the identical dollar amount would be approved instantly for someone else — that gap is the reflex operating, not a genuine assessment of whether the purchase fits the plan.

Budget personal spending with the same formality giving already receives. Many retirees who give generously do so within some rough, informal sense of proportion relative to their plan — a habit built from years of thinking carefully about supporting family. Apply that identical formality, explicitly, to a personal spending category: a specific, named allocation within the verified plan, treated with the same seriousness as a gift, rather than left to compete, informally and at a disadvantage, against every other claim on the account.

The Move: give yourself the first gift of the year, before giving anyone else theirs. Reversing the order — funding one meaningful, plan-approved personal purchase or experience before the year's giving to others begins — interrupts the pattern of personal spending only receiving whatever's left over after every other claim on the account has already been comfortably approved. It doesn't require giving less to family. It requires simply moving personal spending out of last position in the queue.

Notice which identity is being reinforced, and build a competing one deliberately. If a lifetime of being "the provider" has left no equivalent internal permission for "the person who treats themselves well," that second identity can be built the same way the first one was — through repetition. Each time a personal purchase is actually completed rather than declined, deliberately name it, even briefly, as evidence of exactly that identity: not indulgence, but a version of self-respect that took just as long to earn as the provider identity did.

Notice the identical dollar amount test, deliberately, before every deferred personal purchase. Before declining something for yourself, write down what you'd say if a family member asked for the exact same amount for a comparable purpose. If the honest, immediate answer would be yes, treat your own hesitation as data about the category rather than data about the purchase — the purchase already passed the only test that actually matters, which is whether your verified plan can absorb it.

Borrow the exact script that already works, and redirect it toward yourself. “What a father does” is a powerful, pre-approved phrase precisely because it exists and gets invoked without hesitation. Build the equivalent phrase for personal spending, deliberately, and use it the same way: “what a man who worked with his hands for forty years owes his own back” is not a lesser claim than the one that authorized two free engine repairs. It simply hasn’t been said out loud as often.

The postal worker buys a second fishing rod eight months later — a better one, this time, for a specific trip he’s planned with his brother — and mentions, almost as an aside while showing it to him, that he went straight to the counter without the usual three visits. His brother doesn’t say anything about it directly. He just notices, the way people notice a small, real change in someone they’ve known a long time, and lets it be exactly as unremarkable as it now, finally, actually is.

The mechanic finally replaces the recliner on a Saturday, driving to the store himself rather than waiting for his wife to bring it up again, and reports, that first evening, sitting in it for a full two hours without the familiar ache setting in around minute twenty. He mentions to her, almost sheepishly, that he'd apparently been willing to spend four figures twice on his son's car without a second thought and had needed a direct question from her to spend a fraction of that on his own back — a gap he says, out loud, sounds a little ridiculous now that he's actually said it.

The Rule to Remember: the money you give away without hesitation and the money you can't bring yourself to spend on yourself are the same money, from the same account, defended by the same plan — the only difference is which one you decided, a long time ago, you were allowed to want.

Chapter 9 — The Habit That Forgot Its Purpose

A retired bakery owner, who spent thirty-one years opening her shop before dawn and running its finances with meticulous, hard-won discipline, retires with a comfortable and thoroughly verified nest egg — and continues, without any conscious decision to do so, putting a fixed sum into savings every single month, exactly as she did throughout her working years, despite no longer having a business to fund, a staff to cover, or any future contribution the money is meaningfully building toward. When her accountant points this out at their annual review — noting, gently, that she's essentially still running her old savings rate on top of an already well-funded retirement, effectively saving money she has no remaining reason to accumulate — she's genuinely surprised. She hadn't decided to keep doing it. She'd simply never decided to stop.

A retired insurance adjuster describes an almost identical pattern with a specific, telling detail: he still clips coupons, every week, out of habit built across decades of careful household budgeting during years when his family's finances genuinely required that level of attention. He now applies the coupons to a grocery bill his verified retirement plan could easily absorb without any discount at all, spending, by his own rough estimate, more time and mental energy clipping and organizing the coupons than the actual savings are worth in any practical sense. When his daughter asks, half-joking, why he still bothers, he says, simply, that it's "just what he does" — a complete and honest answer, and also, on reflection, not really an answer to the actual question she was asking.

A retired long-haul truck driver offers a third example, notable because the habit in question is spatial and physical rather than purely financial. For thirty years, fuel and food costs on the road were a real, closely tracked expense, and he developed a specific, ingrained habit of driving an extra fifteen minutes out of his way to reach a particular discount gas station rather than using one closer to wherever he happened to be. He still does this, every week, in retirement, in a car that uses a small fraction of the fuel his old truck did, for a discount that now amounts to a few dollars, spending more in time and wear on his own car getting there than he actually saves. When his daughter does the rough math for him one afternoon, he's genuinely startled — not upset, just surprised, the way a person is surprised to realize a habit they never once reconsidered had quietly stopped making sense years before anyone pointed it out.

What's actually happening

All three of these patterns point to something distinct from every mechanism covered so far in this book — not loss aversion, not identity threat, not moral coding of spending categories, but simple, well-documented behavioral automaticity: the tendency for a sufficiently repeated behavior to continue running largely outside conscious decision-making, persisting long after the original goal or context that justified it has changed or disappeared entirely.

The psychologist and habit researcher Wendy Wood, whose extensive body of work spans several decades of research into habit formation, has documented across numerous studies that a substantial portion of everyday human behavior — by some of her research's estimates, close to half of daily actions — runs on habitual, largely automatic processes rather than active, deliberate decision-making, triggered by contextual cues rather than reconsidered goals each time they occur. Wood's research is particularly useful here because it makes a specific, important distinction: habits, once well-established through sufficient repetition, become substantially decoupled from the original goal that motivated them in the first place. A behavior that started as a deliberate, goal-directed choice — saving a fixed sum each month specifically to build a retirement cushion, clipping coupons specifically because the family budget genuinely required the savings — can, after enough years of repetition, continue running purely as a response to its familiar cue, entirely independent of whether the original goal still applies. The bakery owner isn't choosing, each month, to keep saving at her old rate. The behavior has become largely automatic, triggered by the same monthly cue — a certain point in the calendar, a certain balance appearing in her checking account — that triggered it for three decades, running with essentially no reference back to whether the original underlying goal, "build a retirement cushion," has already been fully and completely achieved.

This is worth distinguishing clearly from every other mechanism this book has covered so far, because the fix is meaningfully different. The reflexes in earlier chapters generally involve an active, felt resistance — a specific discomfort that arises at the moment of a withdrawal, a specific dread the mind actively generates. Wood's research on habit describes something with a notably different texture: not active resistance, but simple continuation, a behavior that persists not because some part of the mind is actively defending it against change, but because nothing has yet interrupted the automatic loop that's been running successfully, and therefore uninterrupted, for decades. The bakery owner isn't afraid to stop saving at her old rate. She's simply never had a reason, in the ordinary, uninterrupted flow of her month, to consciously reconsider a behavior that has run on autopilot for so long it no longer registers as a decision being actively made at all.

There's a useful, closely related concept in Wood's broader body of work worth pointing out here: habits are triggered and sustained primarily by stable contexts and cues, not by ongoing motivation or goal-relevance, which is precisely why a change in life circumstance as large as retirement — one that would seem, on its face, like an obvious moment to reconsider every financial habit — often fails to trigger any reconsideration at all for habits that remain embedded in a stable, unchanged context. The bakery owner's savings habit is cued by her checking account and her calendar, both of which look, month to month, essentially identical to how they looked throughout her working years. The context that would normally prompt reconsideration — a visibly different paycheck, a visibly different monthly rhythm — never actually arrived in a form dramatic enough to interrupt a habit this deeply automatic, even though the underlying financial reality changed completely on the day she retired.

The truck driver's fifteen-minute detour illustrates something Wood's research emphasizes specifically about habits tied to physical routines and locations rather than purely mental categories: habits cued by a stable physical context — a specific route, a specific station, a specific stretch of road — are often the most durable of all, because the environmental cue itself does most of the work of triggering the behavior, requiring no active thought whatsoever. He isn't deciding, each week, to drive the extra distance. His hands are turning the wheel toward that station before any conscious evaluation of whether it's still worth it has a chance to occur, the exact automaticity Wood's research describes, playing out in a car instead of a checking account.

It's worth adding a further distinction from Wood's research that clarifies why simply becoming aware of a habit rarely dissolves it on the spot, which matters for calibrating expectations about how this chapter's overrides actually work. Wood's research is explicit that awareness and behavior change are only loosely correlated when it comes to well-established habits — knowing, intellectually, that a behavior no longer serves its original purpose does surprisingly little, on its own, to interrupt a cue-response loop that's been running on autopilot for years or decades. This is precisely why the overrides below emphasize disrupting cues and building replacement behaviors rather than simply asking a reader to "notice" the pattern and stop. Noticing is necessary. It has never, on Wood's evidence, been sufficient on its own.

How to tell the difference. Not every continued savings habit or frugal behavior in retirement reflects this chapter's pattern — some habits genuinely remain useful, and continuing them is simply sensible, not automaticity worth correcting. The distinguishing question is whether the behavior still serves its original goal. If the bakery owner's continued saving were building toward a specific, still-relevant future purpose — a planned major purchase, a deliberate additional cushion her advisor recommends — that would be active, goal-directed saving, not this chapter's pattern. The signature here is specifically a behavior persisting after its original goal has already been fully achieved, continuing not because it's still useful but because it has simply never been consciously revisited.

What it costs you

The most direct cost, familiar by now from earlier chapters, is money accumulating with no remaining purpose, sitting unused rather than funding a fuller retirement, purely because a habit outlived the goal it was built to serve. The bakery owner's continued full savings rate, maintained across years of an already well-funded retirement, represents real spending capacity that could have gone toward genuine quality of life, redirected instead, automatically, into an account that has already accomplished what it was originally built to accomplish.

There's a cost specific to the insurance adjuster's version of this pattern worth noting directly for its own reason: time and attention, not just money, spent maintaining a habit that no longer serves its original purpose. Hours spent clipping and organizing coupons for savings that no longer meaningfully matter to his financial security are hours not spent on the retirement he actually planned for — a specific, if modest, opportunity cost that compounds the same way every other cost in this book compounds, across years of a retirement with a finite and non-renewable number of days in it.

There's a broader cost worth naming, connected to the automaticity itself: a habit running entirely on autopilot, disconnected from active reconsideration, tends to resist even genuinely good information aimed at changing it, not because the person is actively defending the habit the way earlier chapters describe, but simply because automatic behaviors are, by definition, not being actively evaluated against new information in the first place. The bakery owner's accountant can present the clearest, most persuasive case in the world for reducing her savings rate, and that case will have limited effect on a habit that isn't currently being consciously weighed against anything — it's simply running, the way it has for three decades, waiting for something to actually interrupt the loop rather than merely argue with it.

The truck driver's cost is small in absolute dollar terms and worth sitting with anyway, precisely because its smallness illustrates something important: this chapter's pattern doesn't require a large sum to matter, because the actual cost isn't really the few dollars saved at the pump versus the wear and time spent getting there. It's the fifteen minutes, twice a week, spent on a decision his own life stopped requiring years ago, time that belongs, by any honest accounting, to a retirement built specifically to no longer need this kind of unexamined frugality.

There's a shared cost worth stating across all three of this chapter's scenes, because it's easy to read any single one of them as a harmless quirk rather than a real pattern worth correcting: a habit persisting past its purpose rarely announces itself as a decision at all, which means it never gets weighed against what else that same attention, money, or time could have gone toward instead. The bakery owner's unexamined savings rate, the insurance adjuster's coupon ritual, and the truck driver's detour all share the same quiet theft — not of anything dramatic, but of ordinary, recoverable hours and dollars, taken by a loop that outlived the reason it was ever built, simply because nobody had yet stopped to ask it a question it had never once been asked.

The overrides

Interrupt the cue, deliberately, once, rather than trying to argue with the habit. Wood's research on habit change consistently finds that habits are far more effectively altered by disrupting the cue or context that triggers them than by relying on willpower or persuasion to override the behavior in the moment. For the bakery owner, this might mean physically changing the mechanics of the old savings transfer — canceling the automatic contribution entirely and requiring a fresh, deliberate decision to reinstate any portion of it, rather than trying to consciously resist an automatic transfer that keeps firing on its own schedule regardless of her intentions.

Give the freed-up resource a name before you free it. Wood's replacement principle works best when the new destination is concrete rather than abstract; "I'll figure out what to do with it later" tends to leave the old cue with nowhere better to go, which invites it to simply keep firing toward its original target by default. Decide, in advance, exactly what the redirected time, money, or attention is for — a specific fund, a specific weekly activity, a specific person to call — so the old cue has an obvious, ready alternative the moment it fires.

Schedule an annual "habit audit" separate from the financial plan review. A financial plan review typically checks whether the numbers still make sense. It rarely asks a different, equally important question: which financial behaviors are still running purely on autopilot, disconnected from active reconsideration, regardless of whether the numbers behind them still apply. A dedicated, once-a-year audit — walking through every recurring financial habit and asking, specifically, "does this still serve the goal it was built for" — catches exactly the kind of pattern this chapter describes, which a purely numerical review often misses entirely.

The Move: replace the old habit with a new one aimed at the new goal, rather than simply trying to stop the old one. Wood's research finds that habits are generally easier to replace than to simply eliminate, because eliminating a habit leaves the original cue firing with nothing to redirect it toward, while replacing it gives the cue a new, deliberately chosen behavior to trigger instead. Rather than simply stopping the old monthly savings transfer, redirect that same monthly cue toward a new, deliberately chosen behavior — a monthly transfer into a dedicated "experiences" fund, for instance — so the well-worn cue still fires, but now toward the actual current goal instead of the goal it originally served three decades ago.

Make the reconsideration social, not solitary. Automatic habits are, almost by definition, rarely examined in the moment they occur, because examination requires exactly the kind of conscious attention automaticity is built to bypass. Bringing a spouse, a friend, or an advisor into an explicit, scheduled conversation about a specific recurring habit — "why do we still do this, and does it still make sense" — introduces an external prompt for reconsideration that the habit's own automatic operation will never generate on its own.

Ask what the habit was actually protecting against, and check whether that danger still exists. Every one of this chapter's habits was, at some point, a genuinely rational response to a genuine constraint — a business that needed every dollar it could keep, a household budget that needed every discount it could find. Naming that original constraint explicitly, and then checking honestly whether it still applies, is often enough on its own to loosen a habit's grip, because most people carrying this pattern have never actually asked the question directly. They've simply kept running the answer to a question nobody thought to reopen.

Change the physical route, not just the mental rule. For habits cued by a specific location or path, like the truck driver's detour, the fix works best at the level of the environment rather than the level of intention. Deliberately taking a different route, even once, breaks the automatic cue-response chain in a way that simply resolving to "think about it differently next time" rarely manages to do, because the old route will keep triggering the old response for as long as it remains the default path actually driven.

Eight months after her accountant's observation, the bakery owner redirects her old monthly savings amount, in full, into a new standing arrangement: half toward a "someday" travel fund she and her husband had talked about for years without ever quite funding, half toward a monthly dinner out at restaurants she'd always meant to try during the decades she was too busy running her own kitchen to visit anyone else's. She tells her accountant, at the following year's review, that the money moving each month feels identical to before — same date, same amount, same account activity — except that now, for the first time in three decades, she actually knows, and looks forward to, what it's for.

The truck driver, after his daughter's rough math, tries the closer gas station the following week — a small, almost anticlimactic act, he tells her afterward, thirty seconds of driving instead of fifteen minutes, no discernible difference in his day at all beyond the half hour he now has back, twice a week, for nothing in particular. He keeps using the closer station since, not because he made some larger decision about frugality or habit, but because, once broken, the old route simply never reasserted itself the way he half expected it to.

The Rule to Remember: a habit doesn't check whether its job is finished before it keeps running — you have to check for it, on purpose, or it will keep doing a job that stopped needing doing years ago.

Chapter 10 — The Stranger You're Saving It For

A retired copy editor, seven years into a comfortable, thoroughly verified retirement, is asked by her financial planner, almost as an exercise, to describe in detail what she imagines her life looking like ten years from now, at seventy-eight, if she spent her retirement savings at the fuller rate the plan actually supports. She struggles, genuinely, to produce a vivid answer. She can describe, in precise and confident detail, what happens to the account balance under different withdrawal scenarios — decades of professional editing work trained her to track numbers with real rigor. What she cannot easily produce is a specific, felt sense of the person actually living inside those numbers ten years from now — what that version of her wants, needs, would actually enjoy, what a good day looks like for her. The seventy-eight-year-old version of herself is, when she's honest about it, someone she can describe financially but can't quite picture as a person, and money that's being saved for a person you can't quite picture tends, she notices, to feel a great deal harder to release than money you can clearly picture yourself, right now, using.

A retired plumber describes a related but distinct version of the same gap. He has, over years of retirement, developed a habit of describing his unspent savings, almost reflexively, as being "for later" — a phrase that sounds concrete but, examined closely, describes nothing specific at all. When his wife asks him, directly, what "later" actually looks like — what he imagines himself doing with the money, at what age, under what circumstances — he doesn't have a real answer. "Later" isn't a plan. It's a placeholder, standing in for a future self he has never actually taken the time to imagine in any real detail, and money being defended on behalf of an unimagined placeholder turns out to be even easier to keep never spending than money being defended against a specific, named risk.

A retired architect offers a third variation worth including, because his version reveals something the other two don't fully capture on their own: an active, specific mental image of his future self that turns out, on inspection, to be inaccurate rather than merely vague. He imagines his eighty-year-old self clearly enough — he can describe him in detail — but the image he's built is of someone frailer, more limited, and more anxious than any actual eighty-year-old in his own extended family has ever turned out to be, including his own father, who traveled internationally well into his eighties. He has been saving and restricting his current spending specifically to protect this imagined, more fragile future self, without ever checking that image against the real, available evidence of what eighty has actually tended to look like for people in his own life.

What's actually happening

All three of these patterns point to a mechanism documented by the psychologist Hal Hershfield across a substantial and genuinely striking body of research, much of it using neuroimaging to study how people actually process thoughts about their future selves. Hershfield's research, published across numerous papers from the late 2000s onward, has found something specific and important: when people are asked to think about their future selves, the pattern of brain activity closely resembles the pattern seen when people think about a different person entirely, rather than the pattern seen when people think about their current, present self. Hershfield and his collaborators have termed this phenomenon a lack of "future self-continuity" — a psychological and, in some of his research, measurably neurological sense in which one's future self is processed less like an extension of one's current identity and more like a stranger, someone related to you but not, in the moment of decision-making, fully identified with.

This research, notably, was developed substantially in the context of retirement saving, not retirement spending — Hershfield's studies have found that people with weaker future self-continuity save less for retirement, because sacrificing money now for a "stranger's" benefit later carries less motivational pull than sacrificing it for your own clearly identified future self. This book's application of the same mechanism runs in the opposite direction, and it's worth being precise about why: for a retiree who has already successfully saved, the same weak future self-continuity that once made saving harder now, paradoxically, makes spending harder too, for a related but distinct reason. If the retiree's future self at seventy-eight, eighty-five, or ninety-two is processed as something closer to a stranger than a continuous extension of the person deciding right now, then protecting that stranger's resources can start to feel like an obligation independent of — and sometimes in direct tension with — actually living the current, felt life of the person making the decision today. The copy editor isn't failing to spend because she doesn't care about her future self. She's struggling to spend, in part, because that future self doesn't feel vivid or specific enough, in her own mind, to weigh as a real consideration against the present, immediate discomfort of authorizing a withdrawal — and an abstraction, however important in principle, rarely competes well against a concrete, felt discomfort happening right now.

The architect's version adds a genuinely important refinement to the vividness argument, worth saying outright explicitly: Hershfield's research emphasizes vividness, but vividness alone doesn't guarantee accuracy, and an inaccurate vivid image can do just as much damage as a vague one, simply in a different direction. A future self imagined as more frail, more limited, and more anxious than the actual evidence supports doesn't just fail to argue for spending — it actively argues against it, on the strength of a picture that was never checked against reality. This is worth flagging because it means the override this chapter is building toward isn't simply "imagine your future self vividly." It's "imagine your future self vividly, and check that image honestly against the real evidence available to you," a distinction the architect's story makes impossible to skip past.

There's a related and genuinely encouraging finding worth stating plainly from the same body of research: Hershfield's studies have also found that deliberately increasing the vividness and specificity of a person's mental image of their future self — through methods as direct as viewing age-progressed digital renderings of one's own face, or as simple as writing a detailed, concrete description of a specific future day — measurably increases people's willingness to act in that future self's interest, whether the action required is saving more or, by the same underlying logic, actually spending in a way that would genuinely benefit that future self's quality of life. The mechanism runs in both directions: a more vivid future self both saves and spends more appropriately, because vividness is what converts an abstract stranger into someone whose actual, specific well-being the present self can genuinely weigh and care about in the moment a real decision has to be made.

It's worth calling out what makes this chapter a fitting place to close the book, because it draws together several threads the earlier chapters have each traced separately. The plumber's vague "for later" and the copy editor's difficulty picturing seventy-eight are, in a real sense, the underlying condition that every other chapter's specific reflex has been operating inside of: a future self too abstract to advocate effectively for its own actual needs, leaving the present-tense discomfort of loss aversion, moral coding, identity anxiety, and worst-case thinking free to run largely unopposed, because the one thing that should be arguing back on the future self's behalf — a clear, felt sense of who that person actually is and what an actual good day for them would look like — was never built vividly enough to enter the argument at all.

It's worth closing this section with the observation that ties Hershfield's research most directly back to the very first chapter of this book. A vivid, accurately imagined future self and a genuinely functioning reservoir, released deliberately rather than defended indefinitely, are, in the end, describing the same underlying repair from two different directions. Chapter 1 asked you to see the account as an object built for release. This chapter asks you to see the person on the receiving end of that release as real enough to actually deserve it. Neither repair works especially well without the other — an account you're finally willing to draw from still needs a clearly imagined person to draw it toward, and a vividly imagined future self still needs an account willing to actually fund the life being imagined.

How to tell the difference. A retiree who has a genuinely clear, specific vision of a future need — a planned move, an anticipated health circumstance, a family goal with real detail behind it — and is saving deliberately toward that specific vision is not the subject of this chapter; that's concrete, goal-directed planning, exactly what a future self benefits from. The signature this chapter describes is vagueness specifically: money being defended in the name of "later," "just in case," or "when I really need it," without the retiree being able to produce, when asked directly, any specific, concrete picture of who that later version of themselves actually is or what a good day in their life would actually involve.

What it costs you

The cost this chapter describes is, in a real sense, the cumulative cost of every chapter that came before it, viewed from a different angle: years of a well-funded, fully earned retirement spent under-lived, not because any single mechanism failed, but because the future self all of that caution was ostensibly protecting was never built clearly enough to actually benefit from the protection in any way that felt real or vivid to either the present self doing the protecting or, eventually, the future self who arrives to find the caution mostly meant a smaller, more careful life rather than a genuinely better-provisioned one.

There's a particular, quiet grief worth pointing out that tends to arrive for people who eventually do reach the vague "later" they spent years protecting resources for, only to discover the specific vividness never developed on its own with the simple passage of time. A retiree who reaches eighty having successfully preserved a large, well-managed account, but who spent the preceding fifteen years treating every meaningful expenditure as something to defer toward that eventual arrival, often finds, once actually there, that eighty doesn't feel like the moment permission finally arrives either — because the underlying mechanism, an abstract, under-imagined future self, doesn't resolve itself simply by becoming the present. It requires the same deliberate vividness at eighty that it required at sixty-five, and a retiree who never practiced building that vividness at sixty-five has no particular reason to have developed it automatically by eighty.

The architect's cost is worth noting directly specifically because it shows how an inaccurate future self can quietly steal years from the accurate one currently living. Every year he restricts his own travel and activity in service of an eighty-year-old who, by the real evidence of his own family, is considerably more likely to still be capable and active than fragile, is a year taken from a present self who is, right now, more able to enjoy that travel than he may ever be again — sacrificed not for a real future need, but for a future self built from an inaccurate picture he never thought to check.

There's a final cost worth naming across this chapter's three scenes, one that closes the loop back to this book's opening chapter: a present self and a future self who never develop a genuine, felt sense of continuity with each other end up, in practice, treating every decision as a transaction between strangers rather than a single life being lived across time. The copy editor's difficulty picturing seventy-eight, the plumber's empty placeholder of "later," and the architect's inaccurately frail eighty-year-old are three versions of the identical gap, and the cost of that gap is not measured only in dollars withheld. It's measured in years of a single, continuous life spent negotiating with an imagined stranger instead of simply living it.

The overrides

Build a specific, detailed picture of your future self, deliberately, the way Hershfield's research suggests. Not a vague sense of "later," but an actual written description of a specific day — where you are, roughly what age, what the morning looks like, who's there, what a genuinely good afternoon involves. This isn't a creative writing exercise for its own sake; Hershfield's research suggests this specific act of vivid imagination is one of the most reliably effective ways to convert an abstract future stranger into someone whose actual well-being you can weigh in a real decision.

Name the future self specifically when making a spending or saving decision. Rather than asking generally whether a purchase is "prudent," ask specifically: would the version of me at seventy-eight, the one I just described in detail, be better served by this money being spent now or held in reserve. This reframes the decision from an abstract virtue question into a concrete question about a specific person's actual quality of life — a question the vivid future self, once built, can actually help answer.

The Move: schedule a regular check-in with your future self, revisited and updated at least once a year. Future self-continuity, like any relationship, tends to fade without maintenance. A single vivid description written once, years ago, gradually loses its force the same way any mental image fades with disuse. Revisiting and updating the description annually —

does it still match who you're actually becoming, does it need adjustment — keeps the future self vivid enough to keep doing its job in the ongoing decisions this book's earlier chapters describe.

Ask the future self a direct question, in writing, and answer honestly on their behalf. Once the image is vivid and reasonably accurate, put a specific question to it directly: "given everything I now understand about my actual likely health, mobility, and circumstances, what would you want me to do with this money right now, while I'm still the one making the decision." Answering on paper, in the future self's own imagined voice, tends to surface a clearer answer than reasoning about the decision in the abstract third person ever quite manages to.

Check your vivid image against real evidence before trusting it. If your mental picture of your future self is already specific and detailed, as the architect's was, the next step isn't more vividness — it's accuracy. Look at actual people a similar age in your own life, your own family's real health history, real data on typical activity and independence at the age you're picturing. Where the imagined version is notably more limited than the real evidence supports, revise the image deliberately, the same way you'd correct any other belief that turned out to be based on assumption rather than evidence.

Let the vivid future self advocate for spending, not just saving. Most exercises aimed at future self-continuity are built to encourage more saving, because that's the context the research originally developed in. For a retiree who has already saved successfully, the same vivid future self can and should be asked the opposite question just as seriously: what would this specific, clearly imagined person actually want you to do with money that's already secure. Often, the honest answer isn't further restraint. It's live now, a little more fully, on their behalf as much as your own — because the version of you at seventy-eight is not only a claimant on this account. They're also, eventually, the one who has to live inside whatever choices about actually using it get made, or don't, between now and then.

The copy editor spends a full evening, at her planner's suggestion, writing out a detailed description of a specific morning at seventy-eight — the kitchen she imagines, the particular ache in her knees she expects by then, a granddaughter she pictures visiting, the specific, small pleasure of a coffee taken slowly because there's nowhere she has to be. She reads it back the next morning and is surprised by how much affection she feels for the woman in it — not distant, not abstract, someone she recognizes, oddly, as more clearly herself than the number on her account statement ever managed to be. Six months later, she books the trip she'd been circling for two years, not because the arithmetic changed, but because she finds herself thinking, for the first time, about how much the woman in that kitchen would have wanted her to take it.

The architect spends an afternoon doing something he'd never thought to do across three years of careful, protective restriction: he calls his father, still traveling comfortably at eighty-six, and asks him, directly, what an ordinary week actually looks like now. The answer bears almost no resemblance to the frail, limited imagined self the architect had spent years quietly protecting his own future from. He books a trip the following month, not a large one, but the first he's taken purely for himself since retiring, telling his wife it feels less like spending down a cushion and more like finally believing the evidence he'd had access to all along.

The Rule to Remember: you didn't save for a stranger. You saved for yourself, at a later date — and the sooner you can actually picture that person clearly, the sooner you'll stop treating their life as less real than the caution currently standing in for it.

Before You Go

You have, by now, read ten versions of the same underlying reflex, wearing ten different disguises — the reservoir that only learned to fill, the balance that reads as loss even when it's falling exactly on schedule, the budget still calibrated to a paycheck that no longer exists, the invisible ledger sorting your own pleasure into a folder that has to fight for approval, the old job quietly rebuilt in smaller pieces, the advice you trust completely and still can't quite act on, the disaster that keeps almost happening without ever actually arriving, the generosity that flows easily in one direction and dries up in the other, the habit that outlived the goal it was built for, and the future self too faint to argue on his or her own behalf. Ten shapes. One reflex, installed on the same date for nearly everyone who carries it: the day the paycheck stopped and a system built exclusively for accumulation was asked, with no training and no warning, to start doing the opposite.

It's worth saying plainly, one more time, what this book has tried to avoid claiming. It has not argued that all caution in retirement is misplaced, or that you should spend simply because a number technically allows it, or that every hesitation before a withdrawal is evidence of some deep psychological wound requiring diagnosis. Real prudence exists, and a retirement plan genuinely worth defending is worth defending carefully. What this book has argued is narrower and, I hope, more useful: that a specific, common, and almost entirely unnamed gap exists for a great many retirees between what a verified plan actually supports and what actually gets spent, and that gap is rarely about the numbers. It's about a nervous system that spent thirty or forty years learning one rule extremely well, meeting a life stage that finally, after decades, needs the opposite rule instead.

If you recognized yourself in more than one chapter, don't read it as a sign you're unusually affected — it's simply the ordinary shape of how this reflex operates, reaching for whichever channel happens to be available — a budget, a moral category, an old job, a worst-case scenario, a habit, a future self too vague to advocate for anything — in whatever combination your own particular life and history happen to make available to it. The chapters were separated for clarity. The reflex underneath them was never separated at all.

A practical note about pace belongs here, because a book like this one can create a subtle pressure to fix everything at once, and that pressure deserves setting down before you close the cover. None of the twenty composite figures in these chapters resolved their pattern in a single dramatic reversal. The engineer opened the laptop on day twelve, not day one. The pharmacist needed two full years of an unfollowed recommendation before the parallel to her own profession finally landed. The architect needed one honest phone call to his own father before three years of an inaccurate future self started to loosen. Real change, in every one of these composite stories, arrived as a single, specific, repeatable action, tried once, then tried again the next time the same old pull showed up. There is no chapter in this book that asks you to become a different person. Each one asks only for one crossing, one withdrawal, one conversation, one redirected habit, done differently than the reflex would have done it — and then the same small act, repeated, the next time the moment arrives.

And plainly: if a chapter's overrides don't fully resolve the pattern on the first attempt, that's the more common outcome, not the exception. A reflex built over three or four decades rarely dissolves after one successful withdrawal or one honest conversation with a spouse. What changes, usually, is smaller and more durable than a complete cure — the next occurrence of the pattern gets noticed a little faster, resisted a little more successfully, and costs a little less than the one before it, compounding the same patient way the account itself once compounded, slowly, almost invisibly, month over month, until enough repetitions have passed that the change becomes the new default rather than the effortful exception.

Here is the last thing worth saying, and it applies regardless of which chapter landed hardest. You spent decades doing something genuinely difficult: saving, on purpose, past the point of comfort, for a future you couldn't fully see yet. That discipline worked. It's the entire reason there's something real to draw from now. The account did its first job. What remains is not a failure of that discipline, and it doesn't require abandoning it. It requires teaching the same capable, disciplined mind that built the account how to do its second job — releasing what it built, deliberately, for the specific, actual life it was always meant to fund. That's not the opposite of everything you've done so far. It's the completion of it.

Notes & Further Reading

The psychological and economic research referenced throughout this book is real, attributable, and offered here so you can go deeper into any mechanism that felt especially relevant to your own life, rather than taking this book's summary as the final word on any of it.

The life-cycle hypothesis and the retirement consumption puzzle — Franco Modigliani's life-cycle hypothesis, developed with Richard Brumberg beginning in the 1950s, remains the foundational economic model of lifetime saving and spending, and Modigliani was awarded the Nobel Memorial Prize in Economic Sciences in 1985, substantially for this body of work. The well-documented empirical gap between the model's predictions and actual retiree spending behavior — often called the retirement consumption puzzle or decumulation puzzle in subsequent economic literature — underlies the framework introduced in this book's Introduction and Chapter 1.

Prospect theory and loss aversion — Daniel Kahneman and Amos Tversky's "Prospect Theory: An Analysis of

Decision under Risk," published in *Econometrica* in 1979, remains the foundational text for the loss-aversion framework applied throughout this book, particularly in Chapters 1, 2, and 8. Kahneman's 2011 book *Thinking, Fast and Slow* offers an accessible synthesis for general readers.

The annuity puzzle — The economist Jeffrey Brown has published extensively on why retirees underuse annuitization relative to what standard economic models predict would benefit them, a body of research referenced in Chapter 2. This book takes no position on whether annuitization is appropriate for any individual reader's circumstances — that determination belongs to a licensed financial professional working from actual numbers.

Mental accounting and the endowment effect — Richard Thaler's foundational work on mental accounting, including his 1985 paper "Mental Accounting and Consumer Choice" published in *Marketing Science*, and his development of the behavioral life-cycle hypothesis with Hersh Shefrin in their 1981 paper, underlie the framework used in Chapters 3 and 4. Thaler's 1980 paper "Toward a Positive Theory of Consumer

Choice," published in the *Journal of Economic Behavior & Organization*, is the foundational source for the endowment effect referenced in Chapter 4 and Chapter 8.

Status quo bias — William Samuelson and Richard Zeckhauser's "Status Quo Bias in Decision Making," published in the *Journal of Risk and Uncertainty* in 1988, documents the systematic preference for current states of affairs independent of objective merit, referenced in Chapter 3.

Continuity theory and retirement identity — The sociologist Robert Atchley's continuity theory, developed across research published from the late 1980s onward, including his 1989 paper "A Continuity Theory of Normal Aging" published in *The Gerontologist*, underlies the framework used in Chapter 5 to describe identity continuity through the retirement transition.

Possible selves — Hazel Markus and Paula Nurius's paper "Possible Selves," published in *American Psychologist* in 1986, is the foundational source for the framework referenced in Chapter 5 regarding hoped-for and feared future identities.

Visceral factors and hot-cold decision-making — George Loewenstein's research on the role of visceral factors in behavior, including his widely cited 1996 paper "Out of Control: Visceral Influences on Behavior," published in *Organizational Behavior and Human Decision Processes*, underlies the framework used in Chapter 6 to distinguish cold cognitive knowledge from hot, in-the-moment decision states.

Present bias and hyperbolic discounting — David Laibson's research on present-biased preferences, including his widely cited 1997 paper "Golden Eggs and Hyperbolic Discounting," published in *The Quarterly Journal of Economics*, is the foundational source for the present-bias framework referenced in Chapter 6.

Negativity bias — Roy F. Baumeister, Ellen Bratslavsky, Catrin Finkenauer, and Kathleen D. Vohs's widely cited review paper "Bad Is Stronger Than Good," published in the *Review of General Psychology* in 2001, is the source for the negativity-bias framework referenced in Chapter 7.

Habit and automaticity — Wendy Wood's extensive body of research on habit formation and behavioral automaticity, synthesized accessibly in her 2019 book *Good Habits, Bad Habits*, underlies the framework used in Chapter 9 regarding how well-established behaviors persist independent of their original goals.

Future self-continuity — Hal Hershfield's research on future self-continuity, including his widely cited 2011 paper "Increasing Saving Behavior Through Age-Progressed Renderings of the Future Self," published in the *Journal of Marketing Research*, and subsequent work using neuroimaging to study how the brain processes thoughts about one's future self, is the foundational source for the framework used in Chapter 10.

Implementation intentions — Peter M. Gollwitzer's research on implementation intentions, including his widely cited 1999 paper "Implementation Intentions: Strong Effects of Simple Plans," published in *American Psychologist*, is the source for the if-then planning framework referenced in Chapter 3's overrides.

Prosocial spending — Elizabeth Dunn, Lara Aknin, and Michael Norton's research on the psychological benefits of spending on others, including their widely cited 2008 paper "Spending Money on Others Promotes Happiness," published in *Science*, underlies the discussion of giving's independent emotional reward in Chapter 8.

Reference-dependent preferences — The broader tradition of reference-dependent preference research extending Kahneman and Tversky's original prospect theory, including subsequent formalization by economists such as Botond Kőszegi and Matthew Rabin, underlies the discussion in Chapter 2 of how a person's reference point for "normal" account balance drifts gradually over time.

Medication non-adherence — The gap between patient intention and follow-through in prescribed medical regimens is a well-established subject in health psychology and pharmacy practice research, referenced by analogy in Chapter 6; interested readers can find accessible summaries of this research through any major review of medication adherence literature in pharmacy or health psychology journals.

A note on the two economists whose work anchors this book's central mechanism, since Modigliani and Kahneman between them do a great deal of the load-bearing work across these ten chapters. It's worth being clear about the difference in what each contributes, so their combined citation across multiple chapters doesn't read as interchangeable. Modigliani and Brumberg's life-cycle hypothesis describes what a rational plan should look like — smooth consumption across a lifetime, savings drawn down deliberately toward the end of life. Kahneman and Tversky's prospect theory describes why actual behavior diverges from that rational plan — the asymmetric weight given to losses relative to gains, calibrated against a shifting reference point. Neither theory, on its own, explains the pattern this book is concerned with. It's the gap between them — between the smooth plan economic theory predicts and the loss-averse behavior psychology actually observes — that this book's entire argument lives inside, chapter after chapter, in ten different disguises.

A note on how this book uses research, offered in the same spirit of transparency as the rest of this library: none of the studies cited above were conducted specifically on "the retirement instinct" as this book defines it. That framing, and the ten-chapter structure built around it, is this book's own synthesis of well-established underlying research, offered as a genuinely useful lens rather than an established clinical diagnosis with a formal name in the literature. What is well-documented, and what this book has drawn carefully and only from established findings for, are the individual component mechanisms cited above — that lifetime spending doesn't match the smooth pattern standard economic models predict (Modigliani and Brumberg), that losses are weighted more heavily than equivalent gains (Kahneman and Tversky), that behaviors persist independent of their original goals once sufficiently automatic (Wood), and so on through each citation above. This book's contribution is connecting those separately well-documented pieces into a coherent account of a pattern many readers will recognize from their own retirement — a synthesis, held with the same appropriate skepticism you'd bring to any framework attempting to explain something as personal as your own relationship with money.

This book does not offer investment, tax, or legal advice, and nothing in it should be treated as a substitute for consultation with a qualified financial, tax, or legal professional working from your actual circumstances. If the patterns described here are accompanied by broader anxiety, depression, or compulsive behavior significantly interfering with daily functioning, that's a conversation for a licensed mental health professional, not a self-help book. What this book describes is a common, ordinary feature of how a lifetime of accumulation-focused habits meets a life stage that finally requires their opposite — not, in itself, evidence of a clinical condition, for the great majority of people who recognize themselves in these pages.

A note on scope, since this book covers considerable ground across ten chapters and it's worth being explicit about what unifies them rather than leaving readers to assume each chapter is simply an unrelated addition to a list. Every mechanism cited above shares a specific structural feature: each one describes a system — cognitive, emotional, or behavioral — that was calibrated under one set of conditions and continues operating, largely unexamined, after those conditions have materially changed. Loss aversion calibrated to a growing account, a triage instinct calibrated to genuine medical scarcity, a savings habit calibrated to a paycheck that no longer arrives, a mental image of a future self calibrated to fear rather than evidence — ten different systems, one shared structural failure mode. Naming that shared structure explicitly, here, is meant to help the ten chapters cohere as a single argument rather than read as ten disconnected psychological curiosities loosely organized under a common theme.

A final note on the case studies used throughout. The civil engineer, the elementary school teacher, the postal supervisor, the accountant, the social worker, the veterinarian, the airline pilot, the nurse, the office manager, the machinist, the travel agent, the court reporter, the university administrator, the construction foreman, the orchestra conductor, the dentist, the librarian, the pharmacist, the Army officer, the hospital administrator, the claims investigator, the real estate agent, the postal worker, the auto mechanic, the bakery owner, the insurance adjuster, the long-haul truck driver, the copy editor, the plumber, and the architect are each a composite, built to illustrate a real and well-documented psychological mechanism rather than to report any specific individual's life. None is a disguised account of a real client, patient, or acquaintance. What is not fictional is the underlying psychology each scenario illustrates — that part is drawn directly from the cited research and held, throughout, to the standard of being real, attributable, and accurately represented.

A note on why this volume uses three composite figures per chapter rather than the two used in some earlier volumes of this library. The mechanism this book describes tends to wear its disguises more variably than some of the other patterns this library has covered — the same underlying reflex can show up as hypervigilant checking, as total avoidance, or as compulsive reassurance-seeking, three behaviors that look almost nothing alike from the outside. A third scene, in most chapters, was the minimum needed to show that range honestly, rather than letting a single pair of examples imply a narrower pattern than what actually shows up across a real population of retirees.

About This Book

The Retirement Instinct is a volume in The Money Instinct library, a series exploring the specific, nameable psychological patterns that quietly shape how people earn, hold, spend, and relate to money — not through generic advice, but through close, honest attention to the mechanisms actually running underneath everyday financial behavior. Where other volumes in this library examine how people hide from their own numbers, underearn relative to their worth, or carry an inherited habit of underspending regardless of circumstance, this volume turns to a narrower and more specific transition: the exact moment a working income stops, and the reflex that transition activates in people who saved, by any honest measure, exactly the way they were supposed to.

This book does not offer investment advice, tax guidance, or specific financial recommendations, and nothing in it should be treated as a substitute for consultation with a qualified financial, legal, or tax professional working from your actual numbers. Its aim is narrower and, hopefully, more durable: to help you recognize a pattern clearly enough to catch it the next time it fires, in your own life, in real time, which is the only place any of this can actually be changed.

This book was written for a specific reader, and it may help to say plainly who that reader is, so you can gauge whether the fit was right. It's written for someone who has retired, or is close to retiring, with a genuinely well-funded, professionally verified plan — someone whose problem is not whether they saved enough, but whether they can actually use what they saved. It is not written for someone still actively building toward retirement and trying to determine how much to save, and it isn't a guide to retirement income strategy, asset allocation, or withdrawal-order sequencing; other resources, including a qualified financial advisor working from your specific numbers, serve those questions far better than a psychology book can. This book assumes the saving is largely done. Its entire concern is the specific, quiet way that success, once achieved, can be almost as hard to actually live inside as the scarcity it replaced.

It's worth saying outright honestly, too, who this book is not primarily for: someone whose retirement genuinely cannot support additional spending, who is living carefully out of real financial necessity rather than reflex, will not find this book's framework especially useful, and applying its lens to a situation actually governed by genuine scarcity would be a real category error. This book has tried, throughout, to be precise about which problem it's actually solving — the gap between a verified, sufficient plan and an under-lived life sitting on top of it — and this is the boundary of that precision.

It's also worth flagging, briefly, how this volume relates to a companion volume elsewhere in this library dealing with a lifelong, standing pattern of underspending regardless of circumstance. That volume and this one can look, from a distance, like they're covering the same ground, and it's worth being precise about why they aren't. The pattern in that book is present at every income level and every life stage, with no specific triggering event required — it's simply how a person relates to money, full stop, as consistent at twenty-five as at seventy-five. What this book describes is narrower and sharper: a reflex that activates at a specific, datable transition, often in people who had a genuinely easy, unremarkable relationship with spending for their entire working life right up until the week the paycheck stopped. A reader who recognizes a lifelong pattern predating any retirement transition at all will likely find more use in that companion volume. A reader whose caution arrived specifically alongside, or shortly after, the end of active earning is in the right book.

If you found value in this volume, the rest of The Money Instinct library explores other shapes this same territory takes — the instinct to hide your numbers from the people closest to you, the instinct to earn less than you're worth, the instinct to live like you're broke long after you stopped being broke, the fear of what your generosity might do to the people you love most — each one a different angle on the same underlying question this library keeps returning to: not how to make more money, but how to stop being the reason it doesn't get to do the good it was always capable of doing.

A closing word on how to actually use this book. Reading it once will give you the vocabulary — ten shapes, one underlying mechanism, the specific relief of finally having language for something you'd only ever felt before, privately, without a name for it. That's valuable, and it's very likely why you picked this book up. But the vocabulary alone won't do the actual work. The actual work happens at your next real withdrawal, your next verified-but-unused spending capacity, your next moment of catching the old rule trying to run the new decision. Consider keeping this book somewhere you'll return to, not filed away once finished but close at hand, so that when the specific discomfort this book describes arrives, you can turn back to the relevant chapter in the moment it actually matters, rather than trying to remember, days later, what you meant to do differently. A book about a reflex is only useful if it's available at the speed the reflex operates — which, as you now know, is considerably faster than most retirement plans ever are.

A note for readers who arrived here on behalf of someone else — an adult child, a sibling, a spouse who hasn't yet picked up this book themselves. It's tempting, having recognized a parent or partner's pattern clearly in these pages, to want to hand the relevant chapter over directly, as evidence, or as an argument. That rarely works as well as it seems like it should, for a reason this book has tried to be honest about throughout: the reflex being described doesn't respond well to being pointed at from outside, however accurately. If you recognize someone you love in these chapters, the more useful move is usually not the book itself, arriving as a verdict, but the specific, low-stakes questions this book has modeled throughout — what would you tell a friend in your position, what does your advisor actually say, what's the smallest version of this you'd be willing to try once. Let the person find their own way to the vocabulary, at their own pace, the same way every composite figure in these pages eventually did.

Also in the Series

Every book in The Money Instinct library stands on its own — read them in any order. If this one was useful, the library continues:

The Money Instinct

The Secrecy Instinct

The Underearning Instinct

The Shame Instinct

The Panic Instinct

The Merge Instinct

The Ceiling Instinct

The Windfall Instinct

The Control Instinct

The Legacy Instinct

The Comparison Instinct

The Enabling Instinct

The Austerity Instinct

The Paralysis Instinct

The Divorce Instinct

The Enough Instinct

The Overconfidence Instinct

The Vigilance Instinct

The Generosity Instinct